Let's Call It Canada

Amazing Stories of Canadian Place Names

Susan Hughes

Illustrated by Clive Dobson and Jolie Dobson

MAPLE
TREE
PRESS

Dedication

For Steven—a good man who knows there's no place like home
(and always and forever my favourite brother!)

Owl Books are published by Maple Tree Press Inc.
51 Front Street East, Suite 200, Toronto, Ontario M5E 1B3

The Owl colophon is a trademark of Bayard Canada.
Maple Tree Press Inc. is a licensed user of trademarks of Bayard Canada.

Distributed in the United States by Firefly Books (U.S.) Inc.
230 Fifth Avenue, Suite 1607, New York, NY 10001

We acknowledge the financial support of the Canada Council for the Arts, the Ontario Arts Council, and the Government of Canada through the Book Publishing Industry Development Program (BPIDP) for our publishing activities.

National Library of Canada Cataloguing in Publication
Hughes, Susan, 1960–
Let's call it Canada : amazing stories of Canadian place names / Susan Hughes ;
illustrations by Clive and Jolie Dobson.

(A Wow Canada! book)
Includes index.
ISBN 1-894379-49-7 (bound).—ISBN 1-894379-50-0 (pbk.)

1. Names, Geographical—Canada—Juvenile literature. I. Dobson, Clive, 1949– II. Dobson, Jolie, 1981–
III. Title. IV. Series: Wow Canada! book

FC36.H83 2003 j917.1'001'4   C2002-904074-4   F1004.H83 2003

Design & art direction: Word & Image Design Studio Inc. (www.wordandimagedesign.com)
Illustrations: Clive Dobson and Jolie Dobson
Photo credits: page 10: CN002824/Photograph courtesy of the Canada
Science and Technology Museum, Ottawa; 44: Glenbow Archives NA-1141-10;
66: Glenbow Archives NA-2566-1; 70: Glenbow Archives NA-2605-1; 86: Mary
Intven-Wallace.

Printed in Hong Kong

A   B   C   D   E   F

Contents

What's in a Name?

Have you ever wondered how your city, town, or community got its name? Probably not. Most of us don't give any thought to Canada's place names until we come across one that's really unusual, funny, or surprising. When that happens, we may ask ourselves, How did it get *that* name?

And you know what? There's likely an answer that we'd find unusual, funny, or surprising! In fact, when you look into the history of just about any place name, you'll get more than you bargained for. That's because every place name in Canada—the names of all the provinces and territories, of every city and town, of all the lakes, creeks, mountains, and valleys, even of the country itself—was chosen for a reason. Poking around to uncover that reason can be an exciting journey into the past, into the people, the landscapes, and the events that made this country what it is today.

This book will introduce you to fascinating place names from across Canada. Read the stories behind these names, and you'll meet some of this country's earliest settlers, its bravest heroes, and its most colourful rogues. You'll find out about place names that have come from Native myths, local legends, and (boo!) spooky ghost stories. You'll discover spots that were named for physical features and local animals, and others that were named by mistake.

Of course, not every place name in this vast country could be included. It would take a whole series of books to do that! Instead, we decided to focus on the most common reasons for naming, and to include in each category the cleverest, funniest, or most memorable names we could uncover. You can either flip through the book randomly, reading sections here and there, or start at the beginning and name-hop your way right through to the end. The choice is up to you! And when you finish, you may want to head to the library or log onto the Internet to learn more about Canadian place names or look for special names you think you would have included here. (There's even a page of resources at the back to get you started.)

When you're done wandering through this selection of place names, maybe you, too, will marvel, "Wow, Canada!"

Naming Canada

Canada has been a country for only the last 150 years or so— but its name first began kicking around more than three hundred years before that. In 1534 and again in 1535, the king of France, François I, sent the explorer Jacques Cartier across the ocean to the New World. On his second voyage, Cartier discovered the St. Lawrence River and decided to follow it, mapping and naming places as he went.

Can you imagine the scene? Gesturing towards the land, Cartier asks his Native guides, "What is the name of this?" They think he is indicating their homes, however, not the country itself.

Canada is on the North American continent. Did you know that the word "america" came from the name of the explorer Amerigo Vespucci, who was believed to have reached the coast of South America in 1497? A German professor wrote a geography pamphlet in which he described Vespucci's explorations. In it, he suggested that this part of the world be called either Amerige or **America**, in honour of the intrepid explorer—and soon everyone was calling the western hemisphere America!

"The name for 'village'?" they say to one another. "He wants to know the word in our language for 'village'?" And they answer, "*Kanata,*" which is the Iroquois word for "collection of dwellings."

Cartier nods, thinking this is the name of the land itself, and he passes the information on. As early as 1540, the name Kanata—and soon **Canada**—was appearing on maps drawn back in Europe.

Well, the name must have had a certain ring to it, because it stuck. But it wasn't always used to refer to the country as a whole. In 1791, the territory of Quebec was divided into Lower Canada in the east and Upper Canada in the west. (You can learn more about how Quebec—and all the other provinces and territories—was named on the pages that follow.) Then, in 1841, the two Canadas were renamed Canada East and Canada West and brought together to form the Province of Canada. And of course, on July 1, 1867, the British North America Act united the Province of Canada with New Brunswick and Nova Scotia to create a confederation—a country. Now this new country needed a name, and although some people suggested possibilities such as Tuponia, Borealia, and Cabotia, the historical name Canada was eventually chosen!

Cradled on the Waves: The Provinces of Atlantic Canada

When we think of Atlantic Canada, we're likely to picture fish and the sea, the rugged landscape of Cape Breton, perhaps the distinctive red soil of Prince Edward Island. But a look back at the origins of the provinces' names will also introduce you to Vikings and Natives, the French and the English, American revolutionaries and Loyalist refugees—and even a house of the British royal family!

Newfoundland and Labrador

Centuries after Lief Eriksson and his Norse crew first set foot on what was to them an unknown land of white sandy beaches and hills sloping gently down to the sea, Portugal's João Fernandes also came to explore the coasts of what we now call North America. It was the early 1500s and he was a *lavrador* (the Portuguese word for a small landholder). When Fernandes came upon Greenland, he didn't realize that it was separate from North America. He named it and all the land down to Newfoundland Tiera del Lavrador, after his occupation. Later, it was discovered that Greenland was an island, and in 1560, the name Lavrador, which had by then become **Labrador**, was shifted to apply only to the mainland.

And how did Newfoundland get its name? Well, in the 1490s, the explorer Giovanni Caboto (or John Cabot) wanted to find a route to the Far East. Financed by England's King Henry VII, he set sail from Bristol on the ship *Mathew* on May 2, 1497. But Caboto never made it to the Far East—there was a continent in the way.

When he stepped ashore on the coast of this unexpected land (there are still arguments about where exactly he landed!), he called it the "new founde isle." And when he headed home and told people of his adventures, the place was noted in British documents as "New found launde." Some say this proves that **Newfoundland** is the oldest existing place name of European origin in Atlantic Canada.

Nova Scotia

Nova Scotia has long been an area in hot dispute. Settled by the Mi'kmaq, the island was claimed for the English in 1497 (by Giovanni Caboto—again!) and for the French in 1534 (by Jacques Cartier, who later also claimed PEI and large sections of Quebec). But neither country was much interested in populating the new land. Britain focused its energies on the fur trade, and the French concentrated on fishing.

By 1605, all of what we now call the Maritimes was known as L'Acadie (or Acadia, to the English). Worried that the area was becoming too heavily populated by French settlers, the British decided to try to reassert their claim. In 1613, colonists from New England went on the attack and were able to drive away most of the French inhabitants.

To ensure the continued safety of this reclaimed territory, the English government decided to encourage settlement. To that end, King James I granted all of Acadia to Sir William Alexander, a Scottish nobleman, in

1621. The land was then renamed **Nova Scotia**, or New Scotland, in honour of Alexander's homeland.

New Brunswick

Believe it or not, New Brunswick was originally part of the colony of Nova Scotia. How did it get to be a separate territory? Well, it actually all goes back to the American Revolution.

The revolution began in 1775 and pitted those who wished for America's independence from Britain against those who wanted to remain loyal to the mother country. Many of those who sided with Britain, called Loyalists, fled to the area then known as Nova Scotia to escape the fighting. And when the revolution ended in 1783 and independence was won, thousands more Loyalists also headed to Nova Scotia because the colony remained in British hands.

The population of Nova Scotia boomed, and so in 1784, the Colonial Office in London decided to divide it into two separate colonies. One kept the name of Nova Scotia. But the new colony needed its own name.

A British politician suggested the name New Ireland—to go with New England and Nova Scotia. But King George III was not pleased with Ireland at that time, so the proposal was turned down. Other names (including Pittsylvania!) were also rejected, until someone finally came up with one everyone could agree on: **New Brunswick**, after the House of Brunswick, an arm of the British royal family.

Prince Edward Island

In 1534, the French explorer Jacques Cartier landed on the north shore of what the Mi'kmaq had been calling Abegweit, which means "cradled on the waves." Cartier didn't realize he was on an island, but other French explorers who came later did. They called the island Île St-Jean, after St. John the Baptist. In 1758, the British gained permanent control of the island and translated its name into English, calling it St. John's Island. At that time, the island was part of the larger colony known as Nova Scotia.

In 1769, local landowners persuaded the British government to let the island become a separate colony. They wanted this newly independent colony to have a brand-new name, and in 1798 the local legislative assembly finally settled on **Prince Edward Island**. This new name was chosen to honour Prince Edward, a son of King George III's and the commander of the troops in Halifax.

Look to the East: The Provinces of Central Canada

We call Ontario and Quebec Central Canada, but is that really fair? Take a look at a map of Canada and you'll notice immediately that, in fact, the western edge of Ontario just sort of comes close to the centre of the country. The real centre of the country is Baker Lake, in Nunavut! A bit confusing? Ah well, that sometimes happens when people get to naming places.

Quebec

Remember Jacques Cartier's trip down the St. Lawrence River in 1535? When he came to the spot where the river begins to narrow, he discovered a village that the Iroquoian-speaking peoples called Stadacona. Over time, this village disappeared, however, and the site was renamed Quebecq or Kebec, which in the Algonquin, Cree, and Mi'kmaq languages means "strait" or "where the river narrows."

In 1603, another French explorer, Samuel de Champlain, was asked to make some settlements in North America. In 1608, he and twenty-eight men founded a village near the spot where Stadacona had been. Determined that this would become the first permanent French settlement in North America, Champlain named the village the Habitation ("building") of Quebec. The village soon became the hub of the new colony of New France.

The name **Quebec** was used to refer to this village for more than 150 years, a period of great conflict between the French and the British. All that came to an end with the Seven Years' War (1756–63), when France finally yielded New France to Britain.

But the end of that war was not the end of the changes to Quebec.

In 1774, a British statute enlarged the boundaries of the original habitation. Soon, thousands of Loyalists (we met them in New Brunswick, remember?) were flooding into the territory, and in 1791, the British government decided to redraw the boundaries again, creating Lower Canada (which would be primarily French-speaking) and Upper Canada (which would be largely English-speaking). Half a century later, in 1841, these territories were united once again, as the Province of Canada, and given a single assembly. Finally, in 1867, the British North America Act was passed, creating the Dominion of Canada and the new province of Quebec. Its boundaries have both grown and shrunk over the years, but the name, first used centuries before, has stuck.

Ontario

The province of Ontario borders on four of the Great Lakes—Superior, Huron, Erie, and Ontario—but it takes its name from the smallest of these. The lake was probably first called **Ontario** by the local Huron-speaking peoples. We know that the word *ontare* means "lake," and *ontario* might have meant "large body of water." When the province was created by the British North America Act in 1867, it was officially named Ontario, and of course it has been called that ever since.

Huron

Ontario

Erie

Ontario— Squared!

One little community near what is now Stoney Creek was named Ontario in 1851. When the official provincial name was chosen sixteen years later, the towns-people realized they had a problem. Their little community was now Ontario, Ontario! The solution? Change the name, of course. Ontario was soon renamed **Winona**, which is the name the local Sioux peoples often gave their first-born daughters.

Manitoba

There is a lake northwest of Winnipeg that narrows to less than a kilometre (half a mile) in its centre. When waves from the lake reach the shore, they make odd noises as they crash against the loose rocks. Some say the noises sound like bells pealing; others say they sound like human wailing. The Native peoples believed it was the sound of a huge drum being beaten by the Great Spirit Manitou. That's why the Cree called the lake Manito-Wapow and the Ojibwa called it Manito-Bah. Both names mean "the narrows of the Great Spirit." When Europeans began settling the area, they used the Native words for the lake, calling it Lake Manitoba. When the province of **Manitoba** was created in 1870, it was named after this lake.

Yoho!: The Provinces of the West

Have you ever taken a close look at some of the place names of Canada's West? Frontier, Conquest, Deception Creek, Desolation Sound—don't images of adventure, hard times, failure, and success spring instantly to mind? Well, here's one more name that also helps define the West: Yoho National Park. Don't get the connection? You see, yoho *is a Cree word used to express amazement and awe. What a great word to apply to all of western Canada. Yoho!*

Saskatchewan

Just like Ontario and Manitoba, Saskatchewan gets its name from a body of water. In this case, it's not a lake but a river—the Saskatchewan River, of course! And the river gets its name from the Cree word *kisiskatchewan*, which means "swift current."

The name probably first made it to dry land in 1882. That's when several new districts were created within a huge parcel of land known as the North-West Territories. But hold on, that's not the same Northwest Territories that we know today. This massive region was formed out of two other territories, Rupert's Land and the North-Western Territory (you can read more about both of these when you turn the page and head north), in 1870. In 1882, when those new districts were created, one was given the name **Saskatchewan**. The boundaries of the district changed when Saskatchewan became a province in 1905, but its name stayed the same.

Alberta

Like Saskatchewan, Alberta didn't exist until 1882—and it wasn't a province then either. The region that we now think of as Alberta was part of a huge area of land called the North-West Territories. In 1882, when those four new districts were created, one of them was named **Alberta**. The Marquess of Lorne, who was at the time the governor general of Canada, chose the name to honour his wife, Princess Louise Caroline Alberta, the fourth daughter of Queen Victoria. In 1905, when the government of Canada established the province of Alberta, it kept its name!

British Columbia

The province that we now know as British Columbia was originally part of a vast area that the British explorer Sir Francis Drake called New Albion. (Albion is another name for England.) When Capt. George Vancouver arrived on the West Coast more than two hundred years later, in the 1790s, he divided the region into three parts and gave each its own name.

The large island that we now call Vancouver Island he named Quadra and Vancouver's Island, after himself and a friend, the Spanish explorer Don Juan Francisco de la Bodega y Quadra. He then named the south coast of the mainland, including parts of northern Washington and Oregon, New Georgia, after the reigning king of England, King George III. And finally he named the central and northern coastal areas New Hanover, to honour the royal house of Hanover.

Vancouver's names, with the exception of what we now call Vancouver Island, didn't last long, however. They were changed as early as the 1800s, when the fur-trading North West Company began to expand its operations beyond the Rockies. One of the company's partners, the explorer Simon Fraser, was given the thankless task of establishing the first European settlements in this dense wilderness. He was the one who renamed the mainland. For the very northern section, he chose New Caledonia, because Caledonia is a Latin term for Scotland, and the landscape reminded him of the Scottish Highlands. The more southerly area he called Columbia, because it was drained by the Columbia River. Eventually, the border between the United States and Canada was fixed, and most of this southern territory became American land. The land left north of the border was then renamed **British Columbia**, because it remained under British control. And in 1871, when the colony became a province, it retained the name.

The **Beautiful Land:**
The Territories of the **North**

It is the land of the midnight sun, of the Klondike Gold Rush and the Northwest Passage, of Robert Service and "The Cremation of Sam McGee," of the search for the lost Franklin expedition and the law of the North-West Mounted Police. It is also towering mountains, rushing rivers, and Canada's first self-governing Native territory. This is the North, truly the beautiful land.

Yukon

Remember the North-West Territories, that huge region we learned about with Saskatchewan and Alberta? Well, the districts created in 1882 were joined in 1894 by one more. That district was called **Yukon**, after the area's major river (the fifth largest in North America). The river, in turn, got its name from the Gwitch'in word *yuchoo*, which means, appropriately, "great river."

In 1896, three men found gold in Yukon's Klondike River (for more on this important discovery, turn to page 84). In no time, more than a hundred thousand gold-seekers had flooded the remote, rugged land, spending as much to get there as would ever be taken out in gold. Largely as a result of this huge influx, the district was made a separate territory in 1898, and Yukon became its permanent name.

Northwest Territories

Although the Northwest Territories has had many different borders and many different English names, the land has always been called Nunassiaq (or "the beautiful land") by the Inuit, and Denendeh (which means "the land of the people") by the Dene.

Most of the Northwest Territories was originally part of a vast region known as Rupert's Land. Named for Prince Rupert, the first governor of the fur-trading Hudson's Bay Company, Rupert's Land stretched from northern Quebec and Ontario to southern Alberta. It was the centre of the fur trade in Canada.

In 1867, the British North America Act created Canada from Canada East (Quebec), Canada West (Ontario), Nova Scotia, and New Brunswick. In 1870, the new country acquired Rupert's Land and an area defined as the North-Western Territory from the Hudson's Bay Company. This massive new region was then called the North-West Territories. Over the next few decades, large portions were removed to create Manitoba, Saskatchewan, Alberta, and the Yukon, and in 1905, the remaining land was renamed the **Northwest Territories**. Yet the borders of the territory continued to change, with the most recent adjustment coming in 1999, when the western section was turned into the new territory of Nunavut.

Nunavut

The territory of Nunavut was created on April 1, 1999. It was originally part of the Northwest Territories, and when it was decided to create a new territory, there were many discussions about who owned the land and where the new boundary should be. A group called the Inuit Tapirisat of Canada, which represents Inuit Canadians, asked the federal government to divide the Northwest Territories into its eastern and western sections. The Inuit would have claim to the eastern section, and the western section would continue to be called the Northwest Territories. When the territory's residents voted in favour of the new boundaries and the Nunavut Land Claims Agreement was signed, it was only a matter of time before the new territory came into existence. Because its population would be 80 per cent Inuit, it was decided that it should carry the traditional name for the Inuit homeland. That name is **Nunavut**, which means "our land" in Inuktitut.

Lions, Tigers, and Bears, Oh My!: Places Named for Birds and Animals

Look around! Our oceans, fields, forests, lakes, skies, and treetops are alive with an incredible variety of creatures. It's no wonder that so many places in Canada have names that creep, crawl, fly, and swim.

Animal Crackers

In Newfoundland, there are many places that have obviously been named for birds and animals. There can be no doubt about the origins of **Curlew Harbour**, **Cape Porcupine**, or **Deer Lake**, for example. But what about **Hatchet Cove**, **Nippers Harbour**, and **Doting Cove**? Believe it or not, they're all named for birds and animals too. Hatchet Cove comes from a Newfoundland term for the common puffin (also called a hatchet or hatchet-face). Nippers Harbour is named for that annoying pest that has ruined many summer afternoons, the mosquito. And Doting Cove? It's a reference to the word "doater," which means an old seal.

Soft Body, Hard Shell

It's no surprise that a province with as much ocean coastline as Nova Scotia would have many places named for molluscs. **Cape Roseway**, on the southeastern tip of McNutts Island, likely got its name from the many razor clams in the area (the French word *razior* became "rasway," then "rosaway," and then "roseway"). **Grosses Coques**, on St. Mary's Bay, translates as "large shells" and was named for the many large clams on its tidal shores. And **Ostrea Lake**, on the eastern shore of Musquodoboit Harbour, got its name from the Latin word *Ostreidae*, meaning "oyster."

What's a Seacow?

Visit Prince Edward Island and you'll find **Seacow Head** and **Seacow Pond**. Never heard of a seacow? It's an old term for a walrus. There used to be thousands on the north shore of the island, but by 1839, they had become extinct because of overhunting.

Dip, Dip, and Duck

New Brunswick also has its share of surprising animal names. Would you believe that **Dipper Harbour**, **Lepreau Harbour**, and **Manawagonish Cove** have all been named for living things? A dipper is a species of duck, the words *le pereau* are French for "the little rabbit," and *manawagoneesk* is a Maliseet word meaning "place for clams." Of course, there are some more obvious animal names as well. How about **Eel River**, **Old Sow**, or **Sheephouse Brook**?

Moose Tales ...

If it's moose names you're after, you need look no further than Ontario, the moose-naming capital of the world! It's here you'll find **Moose Creek**, **Moose Factory**, **Moose River**, and **Moosonee**. And if you still want more, there's the town of **L'Orignal**, east of Ottawa, which gets its name from the Basque word for moose.

Ouch!

Hornet Lake, southeast of Childs Lake, Manitoba, was named by a crew of lumberjacks who disturbed a nest of hornets nearby. Axes are no match for angry stingers.

... And Buffalo Tales

What Ontario is to moose, Alberta is to—can you guess?—buffalo! All over the province there are places named for this important animal, which provided food, clothing, tools, and even fuel for both Native peoples and early settlers. The **Buffalo Head Hills**, a rugged area in the northern part of the province, were named this because the animals were so common there. **Buffalo Lake**,

northeast of Red Deer, earned its name because it seemed to look like a buffalo hide stretched out and ready to be dressed. (A small stream running off it was the buffalo's tail!) Then there's the village of **Hairy Hill**, northeast of Edmonton, whose unusual name comes from the buffalo that used to shed their hair on that hill in the spring. But the most famous buffalo place name must surely be **Head-Smashed-In Buffalo Jump**, in southern Alberta. For more than five thousand years, Native hunters drove herds of buffalo towards this prairie cliff. When they got there, the terrified animals would plunge right over the side and ... well, you can probably guess how the spot got its grisly name!

Showing Up in Unexpected Places

One morning, mountaineers on the Battle Range Mountains, in British Columbia, woke up after a night of fierce storms. When they stepped outside to stretch and greet the morning, they saw hoofprints near the side of their tent. A mountain goat must have taken shelter from the storm in the night! The mountaineers decided to call the glacier opposite this site **Billy Whiskers Glacier** after the mysterious little bearded fellow.

That's not the only place in British Columbia with an unusual animal name. There's one unforgettable spot named for the day when a mountain guide's horse fell into a canyon between Peters and Spectrum lakes. The hearty animal didn't die—but it was belly up when it was discovered! From then on, the spot was known as **Belly-Up Canyon**.

And what about **Buffalo Creek**, northeast of 100 Mile House? Surely there were never any of these great prairie creatures roaming the mountains of British Columbia! Well, in fact, this little creek was named by local residents for what they thought was a buffalo. But the animal they saw turned out to be an ox that belonged to a neighbouring farmer!

In the Name of the Bee King

What do you do when your community is named Clarkson, but mail is going to every other town and community with "Clark" in its name? Rename, of course. So in 1876, that's what the community of Clarkson, in Simcoe County, Ontario, did. The new name, Joneston, honours David Alanson Jones. Whoops! That's not Joneston, that's **Beeton**. So how does Beeton honour Mr. Jones? Well, he happened to be the founder of the Ontario Beekeepers Association and was known locally as the Bee King.

Greasy Trails

Kleena Kleene, which is on the Klinaklini River, in the southern portion of B.C., gets its name from the Kwakwala word for eulachon grease. The eulachon is a small fish, laden with oil. This oil was a staple of the diet of the local Native peoples. When the eulachon headed up the coastal rivers in the springtime, the Natives caught huge numbers of them so they could extract their valuable oil, which was primarily used for seasoning and preserving food. (The fish itself was so oily that, when dried and lit, it would burn like a candle!) Any extra oil was sold to Natives living in the interior. The trading trails used to carry this oil inland were known, appropriately enough, as "grease trails"!

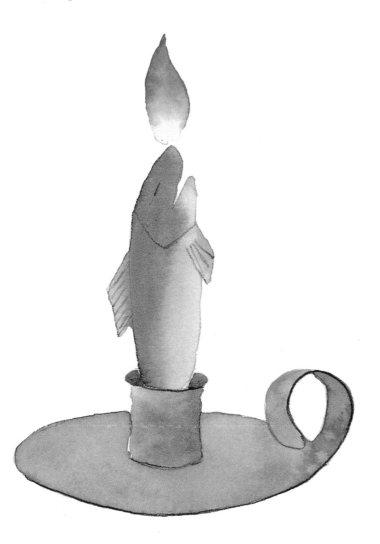

That's Foxy

The town of **Sintaluta**, east of Regina, gets its name from the Assinboine word for the end of a fox's tail. It is near **Red Fox Valley**, which was named for the many red foxes that can be found there. In the valley is **Red Fox Creek**, which flows out and across the prairies. The creek empties into a slough, or a small swampy area, just outside the town, and this slough, from which the town took its name, is the end of the fox's tail.

After You!

Polar Bear Pass, northwest of Resolute on Bathurst Island, is a national wildlife area. It gets its name from the many polar bears that travel through the pass.

Water, Water Everywhere: Places Named for Vessels and Those Who Captained Them

At more than seventy thousand kilometres (43,000 miles), Canada's coastline is the longest of any nation in the world. Hmm, seventy thousand kilometres of coastline ... that sure makes for a lot of coves, bays, inlets, islands, and harbours—not to mention all the many inland lakes, rivers, and streams! Dip into the following place names, a selection of splashy tributes to some of the boats and captains that have sailed and paddled Canada's waters. (Don't forget to strap on that lifejacket!)

Why Not Frances Sound?

In 1787, when Capt. Charles William Barkley first set eyes on a sound, or a narrow channel, on the southwest coast of Vancouver Island, he named it **Barkley Sound**—after himself! His seventeen-year-old wife, Frances, who was along on the voyage, was the first European woman to see the coast of British Columbia.

Two years earlier, a British company had begun trading furs between the North Pacific coast and China. The company had two ships, one of which was called the *Queen Charlotte*, after the wife of King George III. During the summer of 1778, the *Queen Charlotte*'s captain successfully traded for sea otters off the west and east coasts of several large islands north of Vancouver Island. To mark his success, he named these islands the **Queen Charlotte Islands**, after his ship.

The Infamous Captain Bligh

British Columbia's **Bligh Island**, on Nootka Sound, was named after Capt. William Bligh. No doubt you've heard of Bligh, the ill-fated captain of the *Bounty*. Why is there a place in Canada named after this man? Well, long before he was set adrift by the *Bounty*'s mutineers, Bligh sailed with Capt. James Cook on his third expedition to the New World, visiting Nootka with him in 1778.

Land, Ho!

Skinners Pond, south of Nail Pond, Prince Edward Island, is likely named after unfortunate Captain Skinner, whose ship was wrecked near that spot. **Naufrage Pond**, on the Gulf of St. Lawrence side of the Island, was originally known as Etang du Noffrage. This translates as "pond of the shipwreck." The pond was named after there was a shipwreck on the coast in 1719.

Abandon Ship!

The sea can be a dangerous place—if these Nova Scotia place names are anything to judge by! How much hope would you have had of surviving the dangerous seas near one island off Port Joli Point? Not much, it seems, which is why (long before the lighthouse was built) it was named **Little Hope Island**.

On the other hand, **Margaree Harbour**, near Chéticamp, might have been named when a shipwrecked crew *did* manage to survive but had no option except to remain where they were for a while. It was *malgré eux*, or "against their will," but they didn't have a floatable boat! It seems likely that the name Margaree came from this common French phrase.

Malignant Cove, meanwhile, on the Northumberland Strait, was named after the HMS *Malignant*, which was shipwrecked there in 1774, and **The Hawk**, on the southern tip of Cape Sable Island, was named after the schooner *The Hawk*. **Spanish Ship Bay**, on the north side of Liscomb Harbour, likely got its name when a Spanish ship wrecked there, and **Scots Bay**, on the west side of Blomidon, was named when a shipwreck placed a boatload of Scottish immigrants on the shore in 1764.

Can You Canoe?

Ontario may not have any ocean coastline, but it does have almost 177,000 square kilometres (68,000 square miles) of lakes and rivers. That is more than one-quarter of the world's *entire* supply of fresh water! It's no surprise that the early Native peoples took advantage of all those waterways and learned to travel them. Why, they even invented a unique type of boat for that purpose—the canoe. Today you see that word popping up in all kinds of Ontario place names. For example, the long, curving **Chemong Lake**, north of Peterborough, is in the shape of a canoe and takes its name from *tchiman*, the Ojibwa word for the craft. And **Canoe Lake**, in Algonquin Park, was named in 1853 by a geologist when his party stopped there for several days. Why? To build a canoe, of course.

... And Can You Carry a Canoe?

If you were canoeing down the Assiniboine River and wanted to cross to Lake Manitoba, you had to carry, or portage, your canoe on your back. Hundreds of years ago, Native peoples, fur traders, and travellers did just that, carrying their crafts over the flat land of the prairies. This area was first a French trading post and then a Hudson's Bay Company fort. Real settlement began in 1851. By the time the settlement had become a village in 1880, people were calling the "prairie portage" by the French name **Portage la Prairie**.

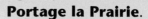

Sweat and Toil: Places Named for Work

Early Canadians performed all kinds of jobs—from harvesting and preparing food, fishing, trapping, milling, gold-panning, and road-building to surveying and studying Canada's history, geology, and botany. There are places across this land named for individual Canadians who have shone in their chosen careers, and some of them have been included on pages 70–73. But here you'll find place names that tell you something about the actual skills, responsibilities, and working lives of the hard-toiling men and women who helped shape this country.

Well, Tickle My Jig!

Want to learn a thing or two about fishing? Well, many of the place names of Newfoundland will certainly treat you to a nibble!

Cod was the main target for the Basque, Portuguese, and French fishermen who sailed to the eastern shores of Canada from Europe, but **Caplin Cove**, north of Carbonear, was named for the smelt-like caplin, a fish that was also in demand.

The **Change Islands** got their name because fishermen would live on these exposed outer islands during the summer and then "change" in the winter to islands where there was better shelter. The name for **Cape Dégrat**, on the Great Northern Peninsula, tells us that this was the spot where fishermen dried their catch on a platform known as a *dégrat*. (Many historians also believe that Cape Dégrat is where Giovanni Caboto first set foot on North America.)

Jigger Tickle refers to the practice of "jigging" for fish—that is, dangling and jerking a line with several hooks and bait attached. And no, a tickle doesn't make anyone giggle! It's a narrow, hazardous strait. **Cut Throat Harbour** introduces us to the cut throat, the worker who had the job of cutting the throats of the codfish in the process of preparing them for salting. (Maybe you'd rather be the one fishing?)

And the fishing lesson doesn't end there! **Killick Island** and **Killick Stone Island** are both references to the killick, which is an anchor made with a stone and wood. **Oakbark Cove** refers to the use of oak to tan fishing nets. (The tanning made them more resistant to rotting.) The oiljackets of **Oiljacket Cove** were flour sacks that had been soaked in raw linseed oil to waterproof them. Fishermen would then wear these homemade raincoats out to sea! **Storehouse Island** must have once been the site of a place for storing fishing gear in winter, and **Tilt Cove** gets its name from the tilt, a temporary lean-to used by fishermen for shelter.

Busy Businesses

Nova Scotia was an industrious province right from the get-go, and these place names prove it! **Glen Dyer**, northeast of Mabou, once had a mill for dyeing, and **Mapletone**, near Springhill, was named after the many maple-sugar camps in the area. **Conquer-all Mills**, on the LeHave River near Bridgewater, was likely a trade name that signified that the lumber made in the mill there was better than any other ("It conquers all"). And **Mill Village**, on the Medway River, and **Milton**, on the Mersey River, were named after the sawmills that once operated in their communities.

A Career High

In New Brunswick, there are several mountain ranges that were named in honour of certain professions, and within those ranges, there are peaks that were named for notable Canadian—or specifically, New Brunswick–born—people who have reached the summit in that particular field.

Southwest of Nictau Lake, for example, you'll find the **Geologists Range**. It contains **Mount Dawson**, which was named after George Mercer Dawson. Among his many accomplishments, Dawson surveyed British Columbia, offering advice on the best route for the Canadian Pacific Railway. He also charted the geology and mineral resources of the prairies.

Historians Range, between the South Branch Nepisiguit and the Northwest Miramichi rivers, contains **Mount Webster**. Mount Webster was named for John Clarence Webster, a prominent physician who, at the age of fifty-six, decided to retire from medicine and begin a new career. He took up the study of history, sitting on the Historic Sites and Monuments Board for twenty-seven years.

Last but not least, there are the **Naturalists Mountains**, southeast of Upslquitch Lake. These include **Mount Ganong**, which was named after the prominent botanist William Francis Ganong, and **Mount MacIntosh**, which was named after William MacIntosh, the first director of the New Brunswick Museum.

That's Life

If you learn how some places got their names, you end up understanding something about the life of the people who named them—how they made a living, where and how they hunted and fished, what crops they grew. For example, frustrated lumbermen in Alberta gave a river west of Edmonton the name **Rivière qui Barre**, or "river that bars." Why? They couldn't use it for driving their logs because it was too narrow. (Another story explains that French pioneers travelling north in 1895 came to a stream of water that barred their way, a *rivière qui barre le chemin*.)

The fur traders often journeyed to the **Birch Hills**, north of Grande Prairie, because they knew they could find bark there. They used the plentiful material to make and repair their canoes.

The Cree peoples named a lake northeast of Edmonton Astachikuwin, meaning **Cache Lake**. This was where they cached, or stored, their buffalo meat before carrying it to their winter camps. It was the Kutchin peoples, however, who named the Thronduik River, which joins the Yukon River at Dawson. The word *thronduik* describes how they drove wooden stakes into the riverbed to trap migrating salmon. Many early miners had trouble pronouncing this word, however. Their distortions came out as "klondike," and the name stuck. The **Klondike River** then gave its name to Yukon's Klondike region.

The name of **Bannock**, a town west of Hudson Bay, Saskatchewan, proclaims a plain but hearty food that was a common meal of the early settlers and fur traders. They combined flour, water, fat, and salt (adding in some blueberries, if they were available), kneaded the dough until it was flat, and then roasted it in a frying pan over a fire. And the village of **Cereal**, east of Calgary? From the time it was first settled, it was a terrific place for hard-working farmers to grow cereal crops.

Hang Tough!

Fort Resolution, which is on Great Slave Lake, south of the mouth of the Slave River, in the Northwest Territories, was established as a trading post in 1815. At the time, it was the most northerly Hudson's Bay Company post. It was named Resolution because it was believed that anyone working and living in the harsh northern conditions needed lots of resolve to survive!

Caution: Construction Zone

Several place names in Yukon originated with work on the Alcan Military Highway, now called the Alaska Highway. Linking Dawson Creek, British Columbia, and Fairbanks, Alaska, the highway was built during the Second World War as a response to increased Japanese hostilities. It was meant to be an easy way to get troops and supplies to the North in the event of an invasion.

When a young lieutenant was put in charge of setting up a tent camp on Kluane Lake for the construction team, he made the mistake of ordering all the trees to be cut down. **Destruction Bay** might have been named for the windstorm that subsequently swept through the area and destroyed the camp! **Soldiers' Summit** is the spot where the highway was formally opened on November 20, 1942. It is named after the eleven thousand soldiers who, along with sixteen thousand Canadian and American civilians, helped build the highway.

Going for the Gold

The **Hogem Ranges**, north of Takla Lake, take their name from a word that was used primarily during the gold-rush days in British Columbia. (To learn more about gold rushes, turn to page 83.) A hogem was someone who would "hog them"—"them" being supplies or goods. A trader was called a hogem when he charged incredibly high prices for his wares— and he was the only one around selling them! And that's not the only place name that tells us how rough life could be during the gold rush. The word "lightning" was once American slang for hard work. When the men who discovered one British Columbia creek were having difficulty climbing down the steep slopes to reach it, they decided the appropriate name for it was **Lightning Creek**.

Dazed and Confused: Misspellings, Mispronunciations, and Plain Old Misnamings

In Canada, you can paddle down Mistake River, camp by the shores of Wrong Lake, or explore the scenery of the Unnamed Bay. They tried their best, but sometimes our place-namers just got it wrong. Read on to learn more about some of the spots that got their names because of all types of misses—mistakes, mispronunciations, and misspellings!

People Power

Moncton is a bit of an unusual name, isn't it? Well, not if you know that the New Brunswick city was named for Col. Robert Monckton, the British army officer who in 1755 captured the French fort that originally stood on the site. Wait a minute—how did *Monckton* become Moncton? It seems that on some official documents, the "k" in Monckton was left out by mistake. So for almost two centuries, the city was known as Moncton. But in the 1930s, some citizens began to speak out. They wanted to retrieve the missing "k." The city council tabled a resolution that the city be officially renamed. Fine and dandy, right?

Nope. Other citizens voiced their disapproval of the addition of the "k" so loudly that, after thirty-six days, the council rescinded the resolution. Since then, the city has been known as Moncton—without a "k."

The H Is Silent

In 1866, William Plows, a justice of the peace, asked the local reverend to choose a name for their village near Owen Sound, Ontario. "It will be Epworth," decided the reverend, to honour the birthplace in England of John Wesley, the co-founder of the Methodist denomination. But when Plows repeated the name, he mispronounced it, calling it **Hepworth**—and the name stuck!

Mistaken Identity

In 1828, a lumbering foreman named William Haslett thought he'd found Nova Scotia's Sissiboo River, the spot where his crew was to begin cutting trees—but then realized he was wrong. So what'd he do? Named the stream **Mistake River**, of course.

A Rock and a Hard Place

On his third and final voyage to the New World, Jacques Cartier was on the hunt for gold. In 1542, the explorer discovered an outcrop of glistening rock on the bold promontory that is now surrounded by the city of Quebec. Thrilled, he ordered his men to take a generous sample of what he believed to be diamonds. Optimistically naming the area **Cap Diamant,** which means "cape diamond" in French, he set off with his booty to France. But when the "diamonds" were examined by professionals, they turned out to be quartz. The phrase *un diamant du Canada* became slang at the time for a scam!

Name That Tree

Oops! When early French-Canadian explorers spotted some tall "hills" on what is now the border between Saskatchewan and Alberta, they called them the Montagnes des Cyprès, or "cypress mountains." The word *cyprès* was often used to describe Canadian forests, which in fact weren't cypress at all. What the voyageurs were actually seeing were lodgepole pines, but we still call this spot the **Cypress Hills**.

Drawing a Blank

In 1904, when Joseph Schmitt was writing a book about Anticosti Island, which is in the Gulf of St. Lawrence, he noted that there was a bay at its end that was unnamed, or *innommée*. But Schmitt capitalized the "i" by mistake—and when others read his book, they assumed that he had *named* the body of water **Baie Innommée**, or "unnamed bay." This has been its name ever since.

Other no-name physical features in Quebec include **Sans Nom** (or "without a name"), **Pas de Nom** (or "no name"), and **Inconnu** ("unknown")!

Dead Meat Falls?

The village of **Carillon**, on the Ottawa River, and the nearby **Carillon Falls** took their names from an officer of the Carignan-Salières Regiment, which was sent from France in the late 1600s to help protect settlements from Native attacks. The officer's last name was Carrion, and he was given a grant of land on the Lake of the Two Mountains from the French government in 1670. *Carrion?* How did this become Carillon? Apparently, there was a mistake in the transcript documenting the grant, and Carrion was misspelled as Carillon! Actually, *carillon* is a French word meaning "musical bells," which is perhaps a nicer name in the end than carrion, which is an English word meaning "dead meat"!

Saskatoon Berries

When the government of Canada began advertising prairie land at one dollar an acre in 1881, the members of the Temperance Colonisation Society of Toronto couldn't resist. Believers in temperance don't drink alcohol, and the members of this group wanted to start an anti-liquor community in the newly settled lands of the West. So they purchased half a million acres (200,000 hectares) east of the South Saskatchewan River, northwest of Regina, then moved out there with their leader, John Lake.

Lake decided the new colony should be right on the bank of the river. He planned to name it Minnetonka, which is a Sioux word for "big water." But then one of the society members was given a branch of purple berries by a Cree man who had come to the area as a member of a survey party. He told the easterner that the Cree name for the berries was *misaskwatomina*.

The temperance member showed the berries to Lake and tried to repeat their name. To Lake, the unfamiliar word sounded like "sas-ka-toon." Immediately, he decided to name the new colony after the berries, and that's how the city of **Saskatoon** got its name.

Oops!

Wrong Lake, on Manitoba's Poplar River, might have got its name when surveyors bound for Lake Winnipeg arrived there by mistake.

Beautiful Bounty

There is a town in Saskatchewan that was originally named Botany because of the beautiful tiger lilies that grew nearby. But when the town survey was completed in 1910, there was a mistake on the blueprints. Botany had become **Bounty**—and the name stuck!

Deer, Deer Me

The city of **Red Deer** is located midway between Calgary and Edmonton. As you've probably guessed, the city was named after the Red Deer River. But did you know that the Red Deer River was originally called Was-ka-sioo, or Elk River, by the Cree? They named it that because of the large numbers of elk in the area. So how did the Elk River become the Red Deer? Well, when Scottish settlers arrived, they mistook the elk for a type of deer that is common in Scotland. The settlers began referring to the river as the Red Deer, and we've been calling it that ever since.

You'd Better Believe It

In 1912, officials of the Canadian Northern Railway were trying to find a name for a new station west of Timmins, Ontario. The president, Sir Donald Mann, thought it would be a good idea to name the station after the contractor who had constructed the railway, Thomas Foley. But he was told by the superintendent that there was already a station named Foley and another named Foleyville. Disgruntled, the president was reported to have muttered, "I'll name that place Foley yet!" His superintendent sighed with relief and replied, "That will be fine, sir." And that was that—the new station was named **Foleyet**!

Whoops!

Wilby. Ah yes, that's a community near Edmonton that was named after a railway engineer. Or is it? Nope. In fact, through some kind of error—perhaps someone's lousy handwriting?—Wilby was changed to **Bilby**, never to be changed back. Poor old Wilby.

The End of the Line

The settlers of one small town just west of Weyburn, Saskatchewan, wanted to give their community a name that reflected its position as the last point on the railway line. They chose Omega, for the last letter of the Greek alphabet. But it turned out that there was already another place with that name. Because they wanted to alter their choice as little as possible, the settlers simply switched two of the letters—the "m" and the "g"—and they ended up with a name they liked just as well—**Ogema**!

Our Father: Names with Religious Origins

Many of Canada's place names have been chosen to commemorate saints, missionaries, feast days, and religious beliefs that travelled here from across the oceans. In this country you can find a city honouring St. John, a river honouring St. Lawrence, and even a mountain range honouring the Virgin Mary. Want to know more? Read on!

Canada's River

On his second voyage to the New World in 1535, the explorer Jacques Cartier discovered the mouth of a great river that was called the Rivière du Canada. He headed down it, the first European to do so, naming places as he went. Now, Cartier was Catholic, and the Catholic Church honours many of its saints with their own feast days. The day that Cartier discovered a small bay on the north shore of this great river was the feast day of St. Lawrence, the patron saint of poor people, so he named the bay after him. Eventually, the river itself and the gulf that leads into it both took their names from the little bay christened by Cartier. Today we call them the **St. Lawrence River** and the **Gulf of St. Lawrence**.

St. Lawrence River

Gulf of
St. Lawrence

St. John's

Just Capital

It was June 24, 1497, when Giovanni Caboto sailed into the harbour on the east side of Newfoundland's Avalon Peninsula and "discovered" the island for England. Because June 24 was the feast day of St. John the Baptist, the man who baptized Jesus Christ, the harbour became known as St. John's Harbour. Soon, many European fishermen were coming to fish in the bay, and eventually a settlement developed there. It was called **St. John's**, after the bay. St. John's became the first incorporated city in the colony of Newfoundland in 1888, and when Newfoundland joined Canada in 1949, it was chosen to be the capital of the new province.

Pilgrim's Progress

In 1811, Benjamin Kohlmeister and George Kmoch, two Moravian missionaries from Europe, travelled up Quebec's Rivière Koksoak (*koksoak* is Inuktitut for "big river"), south of Ungava Bay, looking for a place to establish a church mission. When they reached a widening of the river, they named it Unity Bay. They found an Inuit camp on the east shore, and that was where they decided to set up their mission, naming it Pilgerruh, which is Czechoslovakian for "pilgrim's rest." Although this spot later became a Hudson's Bay Company trading post and was renamed Fort Chimo, it has since 1979 been called **Kuujjuaq** (which is the modern form of Koksoak). It is now considered the northern capital of the region known as Nunavik.

Saints Come Marching In

Most of the French people who came to settle in Quebec were Roman Catholics, so it's no surprise that there are many places in the province named after Catholic saints. Several towns and villages are named **St-Joseph** or **St-Joseph's**, after the husband of Mary and the mother of Christ. There are many place names that also honour Mary (also called Our Lady), such as **Ville-Marie**, **Notre-Dame-de-Bon-Secours**, and **Monts Notre-Dame**. Other saints are also represented, including Ste. Anne, the mother of the Virgin Mary, who is remembered in both **Ste-Anne-de-Bellevue** and **Ste-Anne-de-Beaupré**, and many of Christ's disciples, who gave their names to such places as **St-Pierre**, **St-Jean-Baptiste**, **St-Luc**, and **St-Paul**.

This Way to Freedom

In the 1890s, followers of the religion known as Mennonitism first came to Saskatchewan. The Mennonites believed in pacifism, isolation, and self-sufficiency, and this made them the targets of persecution in their European homelands. The promise of land and the freedom to live as they pleased attracted the Mennonites to the Canadian West. In Saskatchewan, they named one hamlet **Mennon**, after the founder of their group, Menno Simons.

There's Oil There!

In 1890, the surveyor Edgar Dewdney established a Dominion Telegraph station just south of Edmonton. The spot, which was the western terminal of a telegraph line that originated in the Hudson's Bay Company's Fort Garry, needed a name, so Dewdney decided to call it **Leduc**, after Father Hippolyte Leduc. Born in 1842, Father Leduc came to Canada from France and studied to be a missionary in the Oblate Order. In 1867, he arrived in the Edmonton area. He quickly learned to speak Cree and spent much of his time working with the Cree peoples. Today he is remembered for his pioneering work among Natives.

Leduc became a village in 1899 and a town in 1906. After the Second World War, prospectors began drilling for oil nearby. Having endured 133 dry holes, they finally struck oil in February 1947. Eventually, twelve hundred active wells were drilled. The Alberta oil boom was on! Soon, the province was an economic and political powerhouse in Canada, although today most of the Leduc oilfield has been depleted.

Record-breaker

They say that **Mount St. Elias**, one of the mountains in the St. Elias range on the Alaska-Canada border, is *first* in Alaska, *second* in Canada, and *fourth* on the North American continent. Want an explanation?

Okay, here's the *first*: When the Danish explorer Vitus Bering saw the mountain in 1747, it was the official European discovery of the Alaska mainland—that is, the *first* sighting. The mountain was named by nineteenth-century mapmakers after Cape St. Elias, which is on the tip of Kayak Island in Alaska. The cape, in turn, had been named by Bering when he "discovered" it on St. Elias's Day in 1741.

Here's the *second*: Mount St. Elias, at 5,489 metres (18,008 feet), is the second-highest mountain in Canada, just behind nearby Mount Logan, which reaches an immense 5,959 metres (19,550 feet).

And the *fourth*? Mount St. Elias is the fourth-highest mountain on the continent (after Mount McKinley, in Alaska, Mount Logan, and Pico de Orizaba, the highest peak in Mexico). And to top it all off (pun intended!), Mount St. Elias is also the most westerly point in Canada.

Now That's a Houseboat!

It was 1604. King Henry IV of France, anxious that the English not take over too much land in what would one day be New Brunswick, sent Samuel de Champlain and Pierre du Gua de Monts on an expedition to claim more of this contested territory. When the explorers came upon a river flowing southeast to Passamaquoddy Bay, they noticed that it had three branches that formed a cross-like shape. Thinking of the cross (*croix*) on which Christ was crucified, they respectfully named the river the **St. Croix River**.

Many years later, a French missionary landed at the mouth of the St. Croix River on the feast day of St. Andrew, the patron saint of fishermen, and decided to name the site St-André. It soon became known as St. Andrews Point. After the American Revolution, Loyalists (we read about them on page 9, remember?) from New England moved north to the newly created colony of New Brunswick so they could remain under British rule. Some settled on the Penobscot River, but when the international boundary was defined, it turned out that they in fact were still in the United States, and not under British rule after all! When the settlers saw that the area of St. Andrews Point *was* within New Brunswick, they moved there. Some even brought their houses along. Yes, you heard right! They dismantled the structures,

placed them on barges behind schooners, and sailed down the Penobscot River to Penobscot Bay and then on to St. Andrews Point. There they put them back together again—on dry land, of course!

St. Andrews is one of the oldest towns in the province, and today it is known as **St.-Andrews-by-the-Sea**. (And if you visit, you can still see some of the reassembled "homes-to-go"!)

A Pair of Pères

New Brunswick's **Missionaries Range**, a mountain chain northwest of Popple Depot, commemorates several French Catholic missionaries who came to the province in the 1600s. Among its peaks are **Mount Biard** and **Mount LeClercq**. Mount Biard honours Père Pierre Biard, an early seventeenth-century Jesuit missionary in Acadia who ministered to the Mi'kmaq and the Maliseet and, after two years, was captured by the English and returned to France. Mount LeClercq remembers Père Chrestien LeClercq, a Récollet missionary who devised a form of hieroglyphic writing subsequently used by the Mi'kmaq.

By Any **Other** Name: **Names** from the **Pages** of **Books**

Where can you climb Mount Blitzen, swim Lake Cinderella, and paddle Robert Service Creek? Only in Canada, that's where! When they've had a place to name and were in need of some inspiration, Canadians have often turned to a poem, a novel, or a fairy tale for help.

Poor Red Nose!

The ten mountains near the head of the Tobique and Nepisiguit rivers, in New Brunswick, are not officially named the **Christmas Mountains**, but that's what everyone in the province calls them.

Each one of the ten mountains in the range was named by Arthur Wightman, New Brunswick's representative on the Canadian Permanent Committee on Geographic Names, in 1964. He named one mountain **North Pole Mountain** because it was very close to North Pole Stream. (The stream had been named by lumbermen in the 1840s, either because it was so cold there or because it was so far away from any settlement.) Then Wightman named each of the other mountains after a reindeer listed in "A Visit from Saint Nicholas," a poem written by Clement Moore in 1823. There is **Mount Dasher**, **Mount Dancer**, **Mount Vixen**, **Mount Prancer**, **Mount Comet**, **Mount Cupid**, **Mount Donner**, and **Mount Blitzen**.

But that left one mountain without a name. Wightman wanted to call it Mount Rudolph, after the reindeer in the 1949 hit song "Rudolph the Red-Nosed Reindeer," but the committee decided that name was too commercial. Instead, Wightman came up with **Mount St. Nicholas**, and it was accepted.

Flintabbatey Flonatin? Say That Five Times Fast

Many places are named after book titles or authors, but Flin Flon is the only place in the world named after the *hero* of a science-fiction novel!

In 1915, Tom Creighton and some friends found gold near the Saskatchewan-Manitoba border. When the first nuggets were dug out of the ground, Creighton joked that they had to have found the hole where Flin Flon came out and shook his whiskers. What did he mean?

The previous year, Creighton had found a copy of an adventure book called *The Sunless City* while on a portage in Saskatchewan. The main character was Prof. Josiah Flintabbatey Flonatin—Flin Flon, for short. He designs a submarine so he can travel down to the bottom of a lake in the Rockies. After many adventures, Flin Flon returns to the surface through the cone of an inactive volcano, the "hole" to which Creighton was referring.

Creighton suggested that the spot they were digging be named **Flin Flon**, after this eccentric hero. It has been called that ever since.

Winnie-the-Pooh —from Winnipeg Too

Some places have given their names to literature, instead of the other way around. Have you ever read A. A. Milne's stories about Winnie-the-Pooh? Did you know that gentle bear is connected to Canada's Winnipeg?

In 1914, Capt. Harry Colebourn was on his way to Quebec to board a First World War troop ship that would take him to England for military training. As his train was passing through White River, Ontario, Colebourn spotted an orphaned bear cub that a hunter had brought into town. He decided to buy the cub and name her Winnipeg, after his hometown. The name was soon shortened to Winnie.

When she got to England, Winnie lived with Colebourn's infantry brigade and became their mascot. But in 1915, Colebourn was posted to France and had to ask the London Zoo to care for his pet while he was gone. Winnie became so popular with visitors that when Colebourn returned to pick her up in 1919, he was persuaded to let her stay so everyone could continue to enjoy her.

A. A. Milne often visited the London Zoo with his son, Christopher Robin, and he saw Winnie there. When he began to write stories about a bear who lived in the Hundred-Acre Wood with his other animal friends, he chose to name him Winnie-the-Pooh, after Winnie.

Fairy Tales and Magic

Lake Cinderella lies in the northeast corner of Alberta. This lake is named after the fairy-tale girl whose extraordinary beauty is unrecognized at first. The village of **Galahad**, east of Red Deer, was likely named after the famous knight of King Arthur's Round Table. **Lake Merlin** is at the foot of **Merlin Castle Mountain**, northwest of Calgary. They were both named after the magician of King Arthur's Court.

Canada's Poet

Robert Service immigrated to Canada from England in 1894. While working as a banker in Whitehorse and Dawson City, Yukon, Service wrote many famous poems, including "The Shooting of Dan McGrew" and "The Cremation of Sam McGee." In 1968, his name was given to two features northeast of Dawson City, **Mount Robert Service** and **Robert Service Creek**.

What You **See** Is What You **Get:** Names for **Physical Features**

You may be able to picture some of the following spots just by reading their names! Sometimes places in Canada were named … well, for exactly how they appear. What could be simpler?

Hint, Hint

When you have as much seacoast as Newfoundland, it only makes sense to choose some place names that give hints for navigation. For example, **Cape Broyle**, which is northeast of Ferryland, gets its name from the Old English word *broile*, which means "turmoil." This is a reference to the tumultuous waters that surround the cape. On the western shore of St. Anthony Bight, you'll find **Cranky Point**. "Cranky" is an old term that means "likely to capsize," so this place name warned sailors that they needed to be careful rounding the point. And look out here! **Epaves Bay**, off L'Anse aux Meadows, translates to "shipwreck bay"!

Are You Tickle-ish?

Do you know what a tickle is? Careful, it's not what you think. In the Atlantic provinces, a tickle is a narrow, treacherous saltwater channel or strait. Tickles are often difficult to navigate because of their dangerous tides or submerged rocks. In Newfoundland and Labrador alone, there are 250 water features that contain the word "tickle"; these include **Tickle Harbour**, **Pinchgut Tickle**, **Tickle Beach**, and **Leading Tickles**.

Blown Away

Have you ever heard of a "blow me down"? It's an abrupt headland or bluff that rises steeply from the water. You'll find the village of **Blow Me Down**, northeast of Carbonear, on just such a bluff, and if you keep looking, you'll come across at least fourteen other places in Newfoundland with the same name!

Telling It Like It Is

Newfoundland certainly has some of the most colourfully named places in Canada, but sometimes Newfoundlanders and Labradorians just like to tell it like it is. At the entrance to the Nachvak Fiord in Labrador, for example, there is a prominent light-coloured rock that resembles a white handkerchief. What do you think this spot is named? If you guessed **Cape White Handkerchief**, you're right! And **Croque**, which is south of St. Anthony, comes from the old French word *croc*, meaning "boat-hook." It got its name because the bay it sits on resembles a boat-hook!

What to hear a few more? Well, how about **Flat Rock**, northeast of Torbay? Would you be surprised to learn that this settlement grew up near a flat rock? **Fleur de Lys**, on the Baie Verte Peninsula, is named after some nearby rocks that take the shape of a fleur-de-lis (like you'd see on the Quebec flag). **The Topsails**, east of Deer Lake, are four hills that, at a distance, look just like a ship's sails. Each of the four hills has its own specific name too: Fore Topsail, Main Topsail, Mizzen Topsail, and Gaff Topsail. And the name for Labrador's **Kiglaplait Mountains**, north of South Aulatsivik Island, comes from an Inuktitut word meaning "dog-tooth mountains," which is just what the profile of these rugged peaks resembles.

Plainspoken PEI

There are several geographically inspired names to be found in Canada's smallest province. For example, what do you think you would see if you travelled to the body of water that the French named Rivière Platte and we call **Flat River**? Lots of mountains and hills and valleys? Nope, this land is flat. *Very* flat.

And then there's **Sevenmile Bay**. Do you know how far this indentation of the Northumberland Strait stretches between Seacow Head and Borden? If you guessed seven miles, you're correct!

The Three B's

Umiujaq is a village on the Quebec coast of Hudson Bay, 160 kilometres (100 miles) north of Kuujjuarapik. This Inuktitut name comes from the word *umiujak*, which means either "one who looks like bread," "one who looks like a beard," or "one who looks like an upside-down umiak." (An umiak is a large sealskin boat used by coastal Inuit peoples to transport dogs, tents, and other equipment.) It's possible that whoever named the village was looking at a prominent nearby hill that could perhaps be thought to look like bread, or a beard, or even a capsized boat!

Rein It In

Yukon's capital city, **Whitehorse**, gets its name from the rapids in the Yukon River. Long ago, local Native peoples called the rapids Klil-has, meaning "very bad." So how did they get their English name? It seems that the foam whipped up by the churning waters reminded gold-rush miners of the mane of a white horse!

Tea Time

The **Chaudiere Falls** lie between Ottawa and Hull on the Ottawa River. When the explorer Samuel de Champlain first saw them in 1613, he noted that the spray created where the water from the falls crashed on the rocks below reminded him of a boiling kettle. The word for "kettle" in French? It's *chaudière*.

Do you think that's the only Ontario place named for a kettle? Guess again! Because the waves of Lake Huron shaped rock formations into kettle-like shapes, **Kettle Point** in Lambton County was easy to name!

The Yoke's on You!

In farming country, a wooden yoke is sometimes used to join together oxen or other draft animals at the head or neck. The U-shaped collar of this yoke is often called an oxbow, and that same term is also used to describe a horseshoe-shaped bend in a river. The town of **Oxbow**, north of Boscurvis, Saskatchewan (the word *boscurvis* is itself Latin for "oxbow"), gets its name because it grew up on an oxbow of the Souris River.

Obvious in Ontario

Blind River, which flows into the North Channel of Lake Huron, was named by some early Ontario settlers when they noticed that the mouth of the river was completely hidden from travellers passing right in front of it!

Want some other obvious Ontario names? How about the appropriately named **Lowville**? It can be found at the lowest point on the road between Burlington and Guelph, in an area that is nowhere near as high as the neighbouring Niagara Escarpment. And **Key Harbour**, which is just south of the mouth of the French River, was originally named Key Inlet in 1822. It is a long, thin body of water in the shape of—yes, it's *that* obvious—a key.

Or how about **Lake Panache**, near Sudbury? It takes the shape of a feather. Don't get the connection? Well, *panache* is the French word for "feather." And that's not the only descriptive Ontario place name derived from the French. *Pelé* is a French word meaning "bald" or "bare." When, in the 1700s, French explorers first saw one island in Essex County, its eastern side was bald, bare, and treeless. What better name for it than **Pelee Island**?

Don't Butte In

No matter what you're thinking (and it might help to know the word is pronounced "beaut," not "but"), *butte* is actually a French word for "hill." It was likely brought to the prairies by French-speaking voyageurs, and it has left its mark in several place names we still use today. Saskatchewan is probably the butte capital of Canada; it's also where you'll find the plainly named **Buttes**, three steep, flat-topped hills on the north side of the South Saskatchewan River.

Things Are Looking Up

The Beehive, a mountain near Lake Louise, and **Beehive Mountain**, on the Alberta–B.C. border, both get their names because their outlines resemble … beehives! And one peak of **Mount Hat**, also on the Alberta–B.C. border, does look like a hat. But how did **Listening Mountain**, in Jaspar National Park, gets its unusual name? Well, it looks like an ear, of course. The **Pharoah Peaks** in Banff National Park, on the other hand, were named because of their resemblance to a row of Egyptian mummies. Not far away you'll find the **Egypt**, **Scarab**, and **Mummy** lakes!

Brrrrrr …

Nunavut's **Grise Fiord**, on the southern shore of Ellesmere Island, is Canada's northernmost Inuit community. It was named by the Norwegian explorer Otto Sverdup, and it means "pig fiord" in his native tongue. How did Sverdup come up with that odd name? The sound of walruses grunting nearby reminded him of the snorting of pigs! But believe it or not, Sverdup's choice may still be more welcoming than the community's Inuit name, **Aujuittuq**. It means "the place that never thaws out."

For Real?: Weird, Wacky, and Wonderful Place Names

Is there any other country in the world where you can visit such anatomical places as Belly River, Knee Lake, and Joe Batt's Arm? How about wandering down to Punkeydoodles and Skedaddle Ridge? If you're a bit hungry, dig your fork in at Bakeapple Bay, Dinner Place Creek, or Beef Bone Island. Or if you're feeling really out of this world, take off for Lac du Rocket, Mount Venus, or Jupiter Bay!

You Must Be Joking

There's a place on the eastern channel of Placentia Bay, Newfoundland, that was originally known as Famish Gut. Why? When the members of a survey team got there, they had run out of rations and were hungry! Over time, Famish Gut became Famish Cove, and then, in 1940, its name was officially changed to **Fair Haven**. Quite a difference!

Newfoundland must take the prize as the province with the most rib-tickling place names. **Ha Ha Bay** is one that's common—there are five in the province! (Oh, and there's—giggle, giggle—**Baie des Ha! Ha!** and **St-Louis-de-Ha! Ha!** in Quebec, too.) Does "ha ha" mean something funny is going on, though? Not really. It is actually an old French term for a dead end. For example, in Ha Ha Bay, on the tip of the Great Northern Peninsula, there is a sandbank that prevents access to nearby Pistolet Bay.

HA HA!

Why Not Hookey Peak?

Prof. Roy Hooley was wondering why so many of his university students "cut," or missed, his lectures. Then he realized that it was so they could spend more time climbing in the mountains. At his suggestion, a mountain in British Columbia's Garibaldi Provincial Park was named the **Lecture Cutters**.

Record-breaker

Yes, this is for real. The **Lower North Branch Little Southwest Miramichi River** is the actual name for the river that flows southeast into the Little Southwest Miramichi River—and it just may be the longest place name in Canada!

Being Neighbourly?

Emo, west of Fort Frances, Ontario, was named by a fellow called Alex Luttrell. Luttrell knew of a place named Emo in Ireland. He chose that name for the area he'd settled in because he believed that his neighbours didn't have very much education, and he thought this short three-letter name would be simple for them to spell!

But Emo has nothing on one small community between Kitchener and Stratford. It has such an odd name that it's famous! Although no one knows exactly how **Punkeydoodles** came by its unusual moniker, some say it might have had something to do with a local farmer or an early settler. You see, the word "punkey" means "worthless" and a "doodler" is what people used to call a worthless person. The farmer in question was nicknamed Punkeydoodle because he was so lazy that he grew pumpkins and nothing else. Others say that an early settler liked to sing the song "Yankee Doodle," but he garbled the words, so they came out as "Punky Doodle"!

As Easy as ABC

Surveyors named a series of lakes in northern Manitoba, east of Reindeer Lake, after the last three letters of the alphabet: **Ex Lake**, **Wye Lake**, and **Zed Lake**!

Peak, Sneak, and Paddle

At a crossroads north of the village of Norton, New Brunswick, there's another memorable place name. It seems that at this spot, there was once a house blocking the view for travellers on the road. You had to be very careful—peeking out from behind the obstruction—before you could move through the intersection. It's no wonder the location became known as **Peekaboo Corners**.

Or how about this one? When the U.S. Civil War began in 1861, there were some Americans who did not wish to participate. They sneaked, or skedaddled, up to New Brunswick, in particular to an isolated community southeast of Knowlesville. This community of "draft dodgers" became known as **Skedaddle Ridge**.

Ever tried to paddle a canoe against the tide or up rapids? It's hard work, and the reason behind the naming of **Pull and Be Damned Narrows**, in the Letang River, east of St. George, and the two **Push and Be Damned Rapids**, one on the Nepisiguit River and the other on the Southwest Miramichi River.

A Surplus of Pants

Believe it or not, there happen to be an awful lot of lakes in Quebec that, from a bird's-eye view, look like a pair of pants. Pants in French are *culottes*. Get countin'—see if you can spot all thirty lakes in the province with the name **Lac Culotte**!

Bob?

In 1996, plans were well underway to divide the Northwest Territories into two sections: east and west. The eastern section was to be called Nunavut, but no one was sure what would happen to the western section. Eventually, the territorial government set up the Naming the Western Territory Sub-committee. Names suggested to the sub-committee were to appear on a list with the existing name, the Northwest Territories, and from that list a possible new name would be chosen by a public vote.

Some anonymous voices began a "Vote for Bob!" campaign. That's right—they wanted the name Bob placed on the ballot as a possible alternative. Well, before they were able to make their point, the vote was postponed. But never fear! Residents may still be able to rename the Northwest Territories at some future date. Maybe then they'll have the opportunity to consider the name Bob once again!

Out of This World

Some people have looked heavenwards when trying to come up with new and uncommon place names. Sir Peregrine Maitland, a one-time lieutenant-governor who, with his wife, christened many of the places in what would become Ontario, named the township of **Vespra** after the Latin word *vesper*. *Vesper* means "evening," and it also is used to refer to the planet Venus, which is sometimes known as the evening star. And in 1873, a fan of the planet Mars gave the name **Marsville** to a community near Orangeville. And then there's **North Star Creek**, Yukon; **Jupiter Bay**, Northwest Territories; **Mount Venus**, Nunavut; **Neptune**, Saskatchewan; **Mercury Rock**, Nova Scotia; and (ooh, scary) **Black Hole**, Newfoundland.

Cover Your Ears!

Crotch Lake, a cross-shaped reservoir in eastern Ontario, near Perth, was named in the mid-1800s. For a time, people considered its name too racy and changed it to Cross Lake, but it was changed back in the 1960s because … well, everybody called it by its original name anyway, slightly risqué as it was!

Burpee is another Ontario name that might make you giggle. It's a township in the Manitoulin District, and it is actually named for Isaac Burpee, who was the federal minister of customs from 1873 to 1878.

Oops, here's another one—**Butt**. This township was innocently named in 1879 for Isaac Butt, a member of the British House of Commons. Who knew the word would take on a … um, more interesting meaning?

Home, Sweet Home

In 1909, a group of Manitoba settlers found just the right place to live, and they soon had just the right name for their new home as well. They called their settlement northeast of St. Laurent **Ideal**! And when another group of settlers arrived on land northeast of Dauphin, they were confident they would make a million dollars there. So they named their settlement **Million**. T. H. Drayson, meanwhile, the owner of a railway site southwest of Neepawa, named his property **Mentmore**, because he believed his new home "meant more" than anything to him!

Pick a Body Part—Any Body Part!

Knee Lake, an expansion of Manitoba's Hayes River, has a right-angle "knee-like" turn in it. Hence its name! There are also five **Elbow Lakes** in Manitoba, and each of these—you guessed it—twists and turns like a bending elbow. Aierskit Sakahigan is what the Cree called a lake east of Wapisu. Translated, it is **Footprint Lake**. (Get out your atlas and see if it looks like one to you.)

But Manitobans haven't cornered the market on body-part place names—Saskatchewanians have got into the act too. The village of **Eyebrow** can be found northwest of Moose Jaw. It is named for an eyebrow-shaped hill that looms above **Eyebrow Lake**. And you'd better listen up if you want directions to **Ear Lake**, just east of Reward.

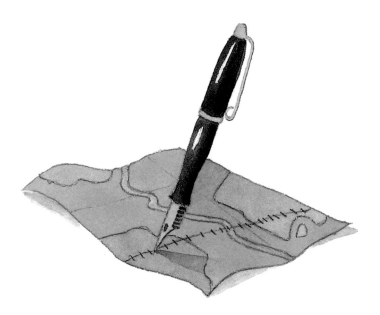

Names That Stuck

You might expect to find a tunnel in **Tunnel Mountain**, which lies east of Banff, Alberta. And in fact, a Canadian Pacific Railway engineer had planned just that for the site. But in the end, an alternative route was found for the railway line—though there was never an alternative name found for the mountain!

A village south of Red Deer, Alberta, also got its name in a rather unusual way. When the CPR was putting a line in between Calgary and Edmonton, the planners were trying to think of a name for a new station. They had no flashes of inspiration—until one of the men happened to drop his fountain pen onto the map. The sight of the nib stuck in the paper was enough to spark an idea, and they called the station **Penhold**.

First Names, Please!: Names from Native Canadians

The First Peoples came to Canada about twelve thousand years ago. They arrived either by land across the Bering Strait or by water in simple boats. Soon the country was full of many nations speaking as many as fifty different languages. They used these languages to name places of importance to them. When the Europeans first arrived, they recorded many of the names that were already in use. Sometimes they reproduced them accurately, but often they altered them to make them easier to pronounce—and occasionally they ignored them altogether. Today, hundreds of years later, many original Native names are being restored.

That's a Mouthful

A portage is a place where a canoe or other small boat is carried from one body of water to another. Southeast of Lac Gaillarbois, Quebec, is **Portage Kamushku-apetshishkuakanishit**. *Kamushkuapetshishkuaka-nishit* is a Montagnais word that means "when we take this portage, we stumble over roots." And yes, it is twenty-eight letters long, which makes it—ta-dah!—another of the longest official place names in Canada.

Go Home!

No, it's not an order you might give a straying pup. In fact, **Go Home**, at the mouth of Go Home River, northwest of Gravenhurst, Ontario, was originally named Kewawenashing by the Ojibwa because this meant "direct route back home" (home for them was Go Home Lake). There was a more rambling route home via the Musquash River, but this way was faster. So the name was simply good directional advice!

Trees, Houses, Seals—and a Battle

Many of the names given to places by Natives on the East Coast described important events, key physical features, or what a place was most often used for. Labrador, for example, was home to the Innu and Inuit peoples, and it is sprinkled with descriptive names drawn from their languages. **Napartokh Bay**, south of Hebron, comes from the Inuktitut word for "tree." This bay is found at the northern limit of the tree line. Head north from here and these might be the last trees you see! And then there's **Igluksoatulligarsuk Island**, which is in Deep Inlet. The name is from the Inuktitut and means "a collection of sod houses." Perhaps there was a small village of these traditional homes on the island at one time. **Aspotogan** is the name of the peninsula that extends into St. Margaret's Bay in Nova Scotia. The name comes from *ukpudeskakum,* which is the Mi'kmaq word for "where they block the passageway." This likely referred to a Native method for killing and trapping seals. The name of New Brunswick's **Shikatehawk Stream**, which enters the Saint John River at Bristol, is from the Maliseet language and translates as "where he killed him." It was the site of a long-running battle between the Mohawk and the Maliseet. To finally bring the battle to an end, it was decided that the two chiefs would fight one-on-one. The victor was the Maliseet chief, and the stream was given this name to commemorate the event.

Turning to Stone

A hamlet on the shore of the Beaufort Sea, northeast of Inuvik, was known as **Tuktoyaktuk** from 1928 to 1936. But when the Hudson's Bay Company opened a post there in 1937, it was renamed Port Brabant after the chief factor, Angus Brabant. Then, in 1950, at the request of members of the local Inuit community, the hamlet was given back its original name, Tuktoyaktuk.

What does this name mean? Well, in Inuvialuktun, the word *tuktuujaartuq* means "rock caribou place." The Inuit tell a legend about the Inuvialuit peoples who lived there. They were extremely hungry one winter, according to the story, because they had been unable to find any animals to hunt. Their shaman, who is a person believed to have access to good and evil spirits, was trying to find food for them. Suddenly, he saw two caribou! But the large animals saw him too and began to flee, escaping into the sea. The shaman turned the caribou to stone (sure, no one could eat them now, but by that point, he was probably angry and just wanted to stop them), and there they remained—rock caribou protruding from the sea. The town took its name from this colourful legend.

God Save the Queen

The Cree called the area in Saskatchewan south of the Qu'Appelle River Oskana ka-asateki, which meant "the bones that are piled together." What kind of bones? If you guessed buffalo bones, you're right. Until the 1860s, when the buffalo herds began to shrink, prairie Natives hunted the great beasts. And they didn't use their meat only for food. They used almost every part of the buffalo—their sinews for thread, their hides for clothing and tipis, their dung for fuel, and their bones for spoons and needles. But some bones were left behind on purpose. You see, the Natives believed that as long as there were some buffalo bones left over, the hunting would remain good.

When Europeans first came upon the area, they translated the name Oskana ka-asateki as Pile O' Bones, and in 1882, the North-West Mounted Police made its headquarters there. Everyone soon assumed this would be the new capital of the original North-West Territories. But Pile O' Bones didn't seem a fitting name for such an important place. They had to come up with something new, and it was left up to the Marquess of Lorne, who was the governor general of Canada at the time, to choose it. Lorne was married to Princess Louise, the daughter of Queen Victoria, and he decided to name the capital after his mother-in-law. Hmmm, he mulled. Should it be Victoria? No, that name had already been used. Instead, he settled on **Regina** (which is Latin for "queen").

Later that year, Regina was designated the capital of the North-West Territories. Saskatchewan became a province in 1905, and one year later, Regina was chosen as the provincial capital.

Saamis Stories

Medicine Hat is located about three hundred kilometres (185 miles) east of Calgary. When a railway station was built at the site in 1883, a tent city sprang up around it. Slowly the community grew, and in 1906, it became a city. There are many stories about how it got its unusual name, but all of them centre, of course, on a medicine hat. The name Medicine Hat is a translation of the word *saamis*, which is Blackfoot for "the headdress of a medicine man."

One story says that during a fight between the Cree and the Blackfoot, the Cree medicine man lost his headdress while fleeing across the nearby South Saskatchewan River. Disheartened at being deserted, his fellow tribesmen gave up and were killed. Another claims that when a group of Natives attacked some white settlers, the medicine man took and kept one of the settlers' fancy hats. Yet another story maintains that after a tribesman rescued a woman from drowning in the South Saskatchewan River, the medicine man placed his hat on the brave fellow's head in admiration. And some simply suggest that the town was named for a nearby hill, which resembled—you're right again—the hat of a medicine man.

Which story do you like best?

When the Spirit Moves You

There are many place names in Ontario that originated with local Native legends. Windigo (or Wendigo) was the name given by the Algonquian peoples to a spirit that was said to "take over" people who were weak and make them act in strange or frightening ways. The name of this important and much-feared spirit shows up, in one form or another, in at least twenty-seven places names (yup, that's twenty-seven!) in the province, including **Windigo Lake**, **Windigo Bay**, and **Windigo River**.

Manitou is an Algonquian word for "mysterious being," the unknown power of life and the universe. The Native peoples had many manitous, most of them associated with nature, but there was one that was superior to all others: the Gitchi Manitou. Gitchi Manitou was the great spirit and ruler of all things. The Natives believed that when Gitchi Manitou created the world, he kept the best bit—the largest freshwater island in the world—for his own home. A sacred place to the local Native peoples, that island, which can be found at the top of Lake Huron, was named **Manitoulin Island**, meaning "where the great spirit dwells."

Another Native legend out of Ontario explains that when the great Nanabozho, believed to be half-man and half-spirit, got angry with a particular old woman, or *mindemoya*, he cut off her head and threw her body into a lake. Left behind was an island (now known as Treasure Island). Even today, if you look at this island's outline, you can make out the shape of a woman on her hands and knees. **Mindemoya Lake**, one of 108 lakes on Manitoulin Island, gets its name from this violent legend.

Fish, Anyone?

Dezadeash is a Native-Canadian word that describes a fishing technique used only in Yukon. Pieces of white birch bark are placed, shiny side up, on the bottom of a lake and weighted down with small stones. When curious trout, attracted to the glinting of the bark, come to investigate, they are speared by waiting fishermen. **Dezadeash Lake** and the town of **Dezadeash**, west of Whitehorse, got their names from this tricky fishing tactic!

47

Qu' Appelle?: Names from the French

Ever since Europeans first set foot on Canadian soil, this country has had a proud and strong French heritage. French place names dot the landscape, from the still-thriving Acadian communities in New Brunswick and Nova Scotia, to strong francophone areas in Manitoba and northern Ontario, right through—of course!—to Quebec itself.

The Naming of Acadia

French explorers were the first Europeans to settle many areas of eastern Canada. As early as 1604, Samuel de Champlain and Pierre du Gua de Monts were bringing colonists to **Ile St-Croix**, on the border of what are now New Brunswick and Maine. Interestingly, though, the name given to the first permanent French colony in North America, **Acadia**, doesn't even come from the French language. So where does the name come from?

One theory of its origin points to the Mi'kmaq. The suffix *cadie* (or *quoddy*) is commonly found among Mi'kmaq place names because it means "a piece of territory or land." It is possible that Acadia grew from there.

Another theory points to Giovanni de Verrazzano. He was an Italian explorer in the service of France who, in 1524, might have been the first European to sail the coast of America from Florida to Newfoundland. It is believed that Verrazzano gave the name Arcadia to the coastal area that stretched from Virginia to Nova Scotia. (The original Arcadia was a region of great beauty, a kind of earthly paradise, in southern Greece.) Over time, the "r" was dropped and the name became Acadia. Soon, mapmakers were using that name for the modern-day Maritime provinces.

But let's get back to Champlain and de Monts. On their 1604 expedition, they discovered the **St. Croix River**, which flows southeast into Passamaquoddy Bay. (For an explanation of the river's name, check out page 33.) Champlain also named Ile St-Croix, the site of that first French settlement. But the colonists' first winter there was a disaster. Almost half of the group of seventy-nine died of starvation or scurvy (a vitamin deficiency) before the spring thaw. As a result, the settlement, now Maine's Dochet's Island, was abandoned.

Despite this disastrous first effort, New Brunswick's first settlers became known as Acadians. They developed a society with its own customs, traditions, and language, which was a dialect based on French. Today the northeastern corner of New Brunswick is still called Acadia and is home to a large French population. And we can find evidence of those earliest French settlers in many place names throughout New Brunswick and Nova Scotia.

The Expulsion of the Acadians

Eager to start again in more agreeable surroundings, the French settlers who survived that brutal first winter on Ile St-Croix moved the next summer across the Bay of Fundy to the northwest coast of present-day Nova Scotia. Samuel de Champlain gave the new colony the name **Port-Royal**. The French settlers soon built a habitation there, arranging a series of buildings around a central courtyard.

But the habitation never enjoyed a great deal of peace. It was abandoned more than once and taken over on separate occasions by English and Scottish colonizers. For almost a hundred years, in fact, it passed back and forth between the British and the French, before finally ending up in English hands in 1713. When the English eventually decided to send their own colonists there in the mid-1700s, they realized that something had to be done about the French. In 1755, they began to round them up, preparing to expel them from Nova Scotia.

Not all the Acadians were successfully captured, however. A number of refugees took shelter on the Bay of Fundy coast, midway between Margaretsville and Harbourville, during the winter of 1756. Some members of this group survived with the help of the local Mi'kmaq, who generously supplied them with food. In the spring, they escaped in canoes across the Minas Channel to **Refugee Cove**, which is east of Cape Chignecto. Others in the group were not so lucky, however; with no food or shelter, they soon perished. In honour of their memory, a cross made of beach stones

Nice Car!

Yes, the General Motors car is named after him, but so is a town in southeastern Saskatchewan. Antoine de Lamothe **Cadillac** was, at various times, a fur trader, the commandant of the trading post of Michilimackinac, the founder of Fort Portchartrain (now Detroit, Michigan, home of General Motors), the governor of Louisiana, a prisoner in the Bastille, and the governor of Castelsarrasin, France. Now that's some résumé!

was placed at a site that was eventually given the name **French Cross Point**.

Years later, some Acadians returned to Nova Scotia. Many went to the settlement of Pubnico, southeast of Yarmouth. When Pubnico grew too large, Jacques Amiraults moved farther along the shore, finally settling at the place that now bears his name— **Amiraults Hill**. Others pushed east to Cape Breton Island, putting down roots at **Belle Cote** (French for "beautiful hill"), on the northeast side of the Margaree River. Still others headed for **Grand Pré** (French for "great meadow"), on the shore of the Minas Basin. Today Grand Pré National Historic Park marks the expulsion, a terrible chapter in Canada's history.

The Carignan Regiment

When King Louis XIV took control of New France in 1665 and made it a French province, he knew he had to bring peace for it to thrive. The Iroquois were battling with the Huron (with whom the French were allied), and they had even begun attacking right in the heart of the colony. Perhaps New France would not survive!

In June, the Carignan-Salières Regiment (named after its two commanders) was sent to New France by the king to help boost the fighting power of the colonists. The regiment's soldiers built forts along the Richelieu River, blocking the main invasion route, and attacked Iroquois villages. Is it any wonder that in July 1667, the Iroquois finally surrendered?

In 1668, the regiment was recalled to France, its job done, but four hundred soldiers chose to remain behind as settlers. The grateful king sent hundreds of young Frenchwomen to the colony as brides for the men! Soon, these new citizens were making a lasting contribution to the life, defence, and economy of New France, and many of the regiment's soldiers are remembered in place names that survive to this day.

Capt. Jacques de Chambly was an officer in the Carignan Regiment. (The name Chambly comes from the French phrase *champ de blé*, which means "field of grain.") In 1665, Chambly constructed a fort near Montreal, which is now a village named **Chambly Canton**. Also named after him are **Chambly Basin**, a nearby village, and the Quebec county of **Chambly**.

When his service in the Carignan Regiment ended in 1672, Capt. Pierre de St. Ours was granted a district in the Richelieu County. The seigneury and town of **St-Ours** are named after him. The county of **Berthier**, meanwhile, was named after Capt. Alexander Berthier. He was given a large grant in 1674 for his service in the regiment. **Berthier-en-Bas** was also part of Berthier's package. (*En bas* means "lower," and it refers to the fact that the village was below **Berthier-en-Haut**, the chief town of Berthier County.)

A Courageous Teenager

Verchères is the name of a village and a county on the south shore of the St. Lawrence River, east of Montreal. It was named after Capt. François Jarret, sieur de Verchères, who was granted a seigneury there after finishing his service with the Carignan-Salières Regiment in 1672. Verchères's settlement grew, and soon he had a mill and even a fort to protect his land. But one day in October 1692, when Verchères and his wife were away, the fort was attacked by Iroquois raiders. The Verchères' fourteen-year-old daughter, Madeleine, fired a signal gun to attract assistance. With the help of several local habitants, she was able to defend the fort until reinforcements came. Madeleine became a hero of New France, and there is a statue of her on the spot where the fort once stood.

Fires of Discontent

One thing is clear: relations between the English and the French in North America in the 1700s were anything but friendly. Round-ups and deportations were the order of the day—and that was before war between the two colonizing powers had even been declared. Battles and skirmishes were fought from present-day Vermont to the eastern end of Nova Scotia, with several fortresses changing hands again and again. Col. James Murray was one of the main British combatants at the siege of the French fortress of **Louisbourg** on Cape Breton Island. (Louisbourg was named after the French king, Louis XIV.) After the fortress was captured and destroyed by the British in 1758, Murray was sent on to destroy the Acadian settlements in the Miramichi area (part of present-day New Brunswick). When Murray arrived at Miramichi Bay, he burned the French settlement there, including the homes, all provisions, and the stone church. From that day, the place was known first as Church Point and then as **Burnt Church**.

Just Pas-ing Through

The Pas, Manitoba, is located northwest of Winnipeg, where the Pasquia River flows into the Saskatchewan River. Originally it was a trading centre that held a strategic position among the fur-trade routes. During the time of French exploration, it was known as Le Pas, and later it became known as The Pas. Its name is said to be from the French word *pas*, which means "passage." This was a place where the Saskatchewan River could be crossed easily. The Pas became a town in 1912. Today it holds an annual Trappers' Festival, with dogsled races and ice-fishing competitions. (Sounds like fun, eh?)

The World at Our Doorstep: Names from Other Lands

Have you ever dreamed of visiting Paris, London, or Vienna? How about Delhi or Glasgow or even Moscow? Never fear! You can see all these places, and many more, without ever leaving Canada. And you don't even need a passport!

Waiting in Hope

Gaspar Corte-Real, a Portuguese explorer, is believed to have reached Greenland and then Newfoundland in 1500. He set out on another voyage to the New World a year later, this time exploring the Labrador coast and Hamilton Inlet. But although the two boats with him on that journey made it safely back to Europe, Corte-Real's ship was never seen again. When his brother Miguel went to look for him the following year, he also never returned. A third brother wished to search for his missing siblings, but he was denied permission to go.

Were the two doomed brothers the source of the name for **Cape Spear**, the most easterly point of land in Canada? It seems possible, since the name was originally Cauo de la Spera, which is Portuguese for "cape of waiting." Perhaps the Portuguese ships accompanying Gaspar and then later Miguel waited there for them to return—which they sadly never did.

But how did the name become Cape Spear? Well, the French adapted the name Cauo de la Spera to the similar-sounding Cap d'Espoir (or "cape of hope"), which was then changed by the English to the again similar-sounding Cape Spear.

From Away

Many names of places in New Brunswick were brought by people from other lands. Welsh immigrants from Cardiganshire, for example, settled and named **Cardigan**, which is south of Stanley, in 1819. In 1831, John Hamilton, from the Scottish island of Arran, named the point on Baie des Chaleurs, near Dalhousie, **Inch Arran Point**. "Inch" is a word used in Scotland to refer to small body parts. And in 1872, **New Denmark**, near Plaster Rock, was founded and named by six Danish families. Today it is one of the largest Danish communities in North America.

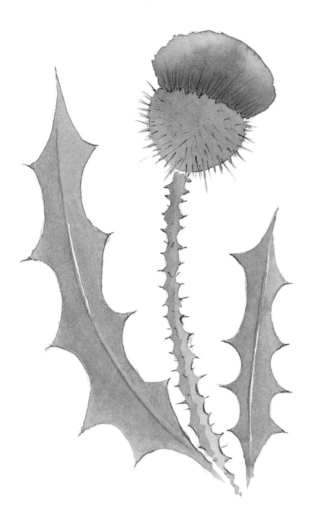

Globe-trotting

Let's have a quick look at some of the spots in Ontario that are named after other countries or places in them. There are **Delhi** and **Elora** (both named for places in India), **Formosa** (named after the island that is now known as Taiwan), **Moscow** (after the capital of Russia), **Paris** (after the capital of France), **London** (after the capital of England), **New Hamburg** (after a German city), **Norland** (after Nordland, a village in Africa), **Odessa** (after a city in the former Ukraine), **Scotland** (after the country), **Upsala** (after the Swedish city of Uppsala), **Florence** and **Verona** (after two Italian cities), **Vienna** (after the Austrian city), and **Zurich** (after the city in Switzerland). Whew!

Through the Glens and Lochs

Some of the most influential settlers in the Maritimes were the Scots. To this day, many Maritimers proudly point to their Scottish ancestry, and you can still find Scottish place names scattered throughout the three Maritime provinces.

The name Nova Scotia itself, of course, is Latin for "New Scotland"—and most Scots would feel very much at home there. They could wander through the glens (any place name beginning with "Glen," including **Glenelg**, **Glengarry**, **Glenholme**, and **Glenora**, comes from the Gaelic for "a narrow valley") and lochs (any place name beginning with "Loch," like **Lochaber**, **Loch Broom**, and **Loch Lomond**, comes from the Gaelic word for "lake"), and think of their beautiful, rugged homeland. There are even places named after

spots in Scotland, like **Argyle**, **New Glasgow**, and **Inverness**. **Barra Glen**, **Barra Head**, **Barra Strait**, and **Barra Grove** are all named after the island of Barra, in Scotland's Outer Hebrides.

Prince Edward Island also has strong Scottish roots. In fact, the Scottish made up half the population of the province in 1798. **Brae**, which is on the Brae River, comes from the Gaelic for "sloping land." And as in Nova Scotia, there are many places with "Glen" in their names, including **Glencoe**, northwest of Montague; **Glencorradale**, near Baltic Pond; and **Glenfinnan**, near the Hillsborough River. The Island also has an **Inverness**, northwest of Ellerslie, and an **Uigg**, northeast of Orwell. **Pipers Creek**, which flows into Tracadie Bay, was named after Michael McInnes, a well-known bagpiper and a member of the Scottish family who originally settled the area.

Hail to Nova Scotia

People from all over Europe (not just the Scottish) settled Nova Scotia—and all you have to do is look at some of the province's place names to prove it! **Aspy Bay**, at the northeastern tip of Cape Breton Island, originated with the Basque people and was named for Pic d'Aspé in the Pyrenees Mountains of France and Spain. And in fact, the name for **Cape Breton** itself probably comes from the Bretons, a Celtic people who live in Brittany, which is a region in the northwest corner of France. The Bretons first came to the shores of the Maritimes in the 1500s. Other Nova Scotia names originate from the French colonial period, including **French River** (there are three of them in the province) and **French Village**, at the head of St. Margaret's Bay. And then there's the Acadian town of **Saulnierville**, north of Yarmouth. This place name remembers the *saulniers*, people who toiled in the salt works back in their native France. Long ago, people sometimes adopted last names that reflected their occupations, and we can see the remnants of this custom in Saulnierville, where to this day many residents still share the surname Saulnier.

There are also several place names with British roots in the province. **Avondale**, near the Avon River, was named after the many, many Avon rivers in England. And **Jersey Cove**, on St. Ann's Bay; **Jerseymans Island**, southwest of Arichat; and **Jersey Point**, southwest of Petit-de-Grat, are all named after Jersey, one of the British Channel Islands.

Remembering Ukraine

Ukrainian immigrants came to Canada by the thousands, especially between the two world wars, and settled all over the Prairies, from Manitoba to Alberta. They brought with them many cultural traditions that are now a treasured part of many Canadians' lives. And of course, they brought some place names too. In Manitoba, northwest of Gimli, you can find **Zbaraz**. It's named after a place in western Ukraine. **Senkiw**, northeast of Emerson, is named after a Ukrainian village near Azliztsi, in Halychyna. And the village of **Komarno**, southwest of Gimli, was given its name by a Ukrainian pioneer, Joseph Leschuk. The Ukrainian word *komarno* means "full of mosquitoes"!

In Saskatchewan, the Ukrainians were also a significant immigrant community. There they named **Whitkow**, **Tarnopol**, and **Odessa**. Why, they even named **Laniwci**, which comes from the Ukrainian word *lani*, meaning "prairies," appropriately enough.

A Little Bit of Heaven

When several communities were established on the west shore of Lake Winnipeg, in Manitoba, by Icelandic settlers in 1875, the area became known as New Iceland. The Icelanders themselves called the place where they first touched land the Great Hall of Heaven, or **Gimli**. Today Gimli is the largest Icelandic settlement outside of Iceland itself. Thousands of people from all over the world visit the town every year for its annual Icelandic festival. **Hecla Island** in Lake Winnipeg also has Icelandic origins. It was named after the Hecla volcano. When Hecla erupted in 1845, it caused great damage—and probably convinced some Icelanders to leave their homeland and move to Canada!

Welcoming the World

Saskatchewanians can be found everywhere from Amsterdam to Strasbourg. Is that because they are such great world travellers? Nope, it's because the world has come to them. Over the years, new arrivals from across the globe have left their mark with place names that you'd never expect to find on the wide-open spaces of the prairie. Dutch immigrants christened **Edam** and **Amsterdam**, both named for places in their native Holland. Germans founded **Strasbourg** and Austrians **Neudorf**. Even the English, the Welsh, and the Irish got in on the act, dubbing **Fairy Glen**, **Glaslyn**, and **Limerick** after places they too had left behind.

A Home Away from Home

Just as in Saskatchewan, people from all over have been drawn to Alberta. Sometimes they have named their new homes in their mother tongue or after places in their country of origin. A valley near Calgary, for example, was named **Bergen** by the Norwegian pioneers who first settled there. Bergen was the original capital of Norway. The community of **Friedenstal**, north of Grande Prairie, was named by a Romanian settler for his former home, and **Banff** was named by developers from Banffshire, Scotland.

German immigrants settled large portions of the province, so many German-inspired names can be found as well. **Bismarck** was named for Otto von Bismarck, a nineteenth-century German statesman, and **Chancellor** was named for the title of the former German head of state. As happened in other provinces, some towns changed their names during the First World War because of anti-German sentiment. The decidedly German-sounding Carlstadt, for example, changed its name to **Alderson** in 1915.

And what about the hamlet of **Pibroch**? Well, although that is a Scottish word for the sound made by the bagpipes, that's not exactly how the hamlet got its name. Would you believe that one of Pibroch's Scottish settlers chose the name because it was the same as his cat's?

After You, **Your Majesty!**: Places Named for **Royalty**

Want to impress a king, queen, prince, princess, or lesser royal? You could bow, curtsy, doff your hat, go down on one knee—or simply name a place for him or her! From Queensland, Queensville, and Queensport to Kingston, Kingsville, and Kingsclear, the map of Canada makes a great royal connect-the-dots (or crowns?) puzzle!

The Queen—Again and Again

Nova Scotians love their monarchs—and none more than Queen Victoria, who gained the English throne in 1837. Shortly after Victoria's coronation, Nova Scotians named **Queensland**, east of Hubbards on St. Margaret's Bay, for her. And there's more. **Queensville**, north of Port Hawkesbury, was named to mark her twenty-fifth year on the throne in 1862, and **Queensport**, on Chedabucto Bay, was renamed in 1898 to mark her sixtieth year on the throne, her Diamond Jubilee (which had occurred the year before). And then there's **Victoria Beach**, on Digby Gut, and **Victoria Vale**, north of Middleton—and at least *twelve* other place names that contain the queen's name in one form or another!

But Nova Scotians are not alone in their love of Britain's longest-serving ruler. Her name appears on the Canadian map more than three hundred times! In fact, no one person has been immortalized in more of Canada's place names than she.

The City on the Mountain

There is an island at the intersection of the St. Lawrence and Ottawa rivers. In 1535, Jacques Cartier named the mountain on this island **Mont Royal**, to honour the French king, François I. At that time, the words "royal" and "real" had the same meaning in French, so soon people were referring to the mountain as Mont Real. The colony that was established there in 1642 was first known as Ville Marie en l'Isle de Montréal. By the 1700s, the name had been shortened to **Montréal**, and that is now the largest city in Quebec.

Charlotte's Story

In 1765, Canada's greatest surveyor, Samuel Holland, divided Prince Edward Island into three counties. Holland gave each county a royal name and also a capital. Kings County had **Georgetown** (named for King George III of England), Prince County had **Princetown** (named for the king's eldest son), and Queens County had **Charlottetown** (named for Queen Charlotte, wife to the king). Charlottetown became the capital of the entire province and was incorporated as a city in 1875.

So just who was Queen Charlotte? Born into the royal house of a small German principality in 1744, Sophie Charlotte of Mecklenburg-Strelitz was promised to King George III when she was just seventeen. The two had never met, and Charlotte spoke no English save for the few words she memorized during her long voyage from her homeland to St. James's Palace in London. But she took her role as wife of the king very seriously, and by all accounts, the two had a happy marriage. In twenty-one years, she gave birth to fifteen children, including the future King George IV.

Sadly, the happiness did not last. In 1788, the king began a slow descent into madness, the result of an inherited illness that also affected Mary Queen of Scots and King James I, and by 1810, he was completely insane. Queen Charlotte was devoted to her king, however, and she stayed by his side, nursing him as best she could, until his death in 1820.

In recent years, Charlotte's ancestry has been traced back to a black branch of the Portuguese royal house. She has been championed by blacks all over the world, who point to portraits and the descriptions of people who knew her as proof that Charlotte was partly black.

In Canada, this remarkable woman is remembered in many place names, including Charlotte County (in New Brunswick), the Queen Charlotte Islands (in British Columbia), and two additional Queens counties (one in Nova Scotia and one in New Brunswick).

Frederick's Town

The capital of New Brunswick was originally an Acadian village on the bank of the Saint John River. Named Ste-Anne, it was settled in 1731. But then, in 1755, the Acadians were expelled. Three years later, the governor of Nova Scotia invited the people of New England, a colony in the United States, to come north and settle the vacant lands. Some of them came to Ste-Anne, settled there, and renamed it St. Anne's Point.

In 1784, more colonists from the United States arrived. They were Loyalists fleeing the American Revolution. That same year, New Brunswick was divided from Nova Scotia. The new colony was given a lieutenant-governor, Thomas Carleton, who had come from Britain to rule in the king's name. All that was still needed was a capital city. St. Anne's Point was chosen, and in 1785, its name was changed to Fredericktown, after Prince Frederick, the second son of England's King George III. Soon after, the "k" and the "w" were dropped, and the town became **Fredericton**. It was incorporated as a city in 1848.

Selkirk's Colony

Selkirk, a town northeast of Winnipeg, was named after Thomas Douglas, the fifth earl of Selkirk and the man behind the famous Red River Colony, established in 1812 at the forks of the Red and Assiniboine rivers (now downtown Winnipeg).

Selkirk wanted the Red River Colony to be a self-sufficient agricultural community, but the original settlers had difficulty growing enough food to survive. When the colonists tried to prevent members of the North West Company, the fur-trading rivals to the Hudson's Bay Company (which Selkirk's family controlled), from gathering provisions in the area, conflict broke out. Life proved too hard for most of the original members of the colony, and the settlement was abandoned in 1815.

Selkirk was not one to give up, however. He named a new governor for the colony and recruited discharged Swiss soldiers who had fought in the War of 1812 to repopulate it. He was heading to the settlement with this group in the summer of 1816 when he learned of the Seven Oaks Incident, a violent conflict between several Métis (supporters of the North West Company) and Robert Semple, the new governor. Semple and twenty of his men were killed.

Selkirk restored the confidence of some of the settlers when he finally arrived at the Red River Colony in July 1816. He distributed land and promised the colonists access to schools and churches. But the struggles did not end there. Locusts destroyed the crops in 1818 and 1819, and a massive flood of the Red River did more damage in 1826. Ongoing conflicts between English-speaking European settlers and French-speaking Métis eventually led to the Red River Rebellion in 1869–70.

For all its troubles, though, the Red River Colony showed the possibilities of mixing different cultural and religious groups. For that, Selkirk is remembered not only in the town that bears his name but also in a **Selkirk Island** on Lake Winnipeg, north of the mouth of the Saskatchewan River.

A Royal Family

The **Royal Group** of the Rocky Mountains is in southeastern British Columbia, north of the Palliser Range. The highest peak, at 3,422 metres (11,227 feet), is named after King George V, and other peaks are named for his wife, Queen Mary, and their children, Prince Edward, Prince George, Prince Henry, Prince John, and Princess Mary!

By George!

In Great Britain, there have been six monarchs named George, and many places in Ontario are named after one or the other of these kings. When a town on the St. Lawrence River between Belleville and Brockville became a city in 1846, it was first called King's Town—after George III. The name was later simplified to **Kingston**. Kingston was the capital of the Province of Canada from 1841 to 1844.

And the large arm of Lake Huron—originally named Mer Douce (or "freshwater sea") by Samuel de Champlain in 1615 and later called Lake Manitoulin—was renamed when it was mapped in 1822. It was christened **Georgian Bay** for the newly crowned King George IV.

Let's Have a Recount

By 1867, the Grand Trunk Railway, which ran from Sarnia, Ontario, through Montreal to Portland, Maine, was the largest railway system in the world. The company planned to stretch its rail line even farther—across the entire country to the Pacific Ocean. It wanted a great name for its western terminus, so in 1906, it sponsored a contest. Contestants were to submit names with no more than three syllables and ten letters; they had the chance to win a prize of $250—which was a lot of money back then. Eleanor MacDonald of Winnipeg was the eventual winner, with her suggestion of **Prince Rupert**. Prince Rupert of the Rhine, a cousin of King Charles II, had been the first governor of the Hudson's Bay Company.

But count the letters in the name Prince Rupert and what do you notice? That's right—there are twelve of them, not ten. Although the railway company stuck with the name, it decided to award two other contestants with prizes for their suggestion of Port Rupert (which, yes, does have ten letters!).

What a Mouthful!

Madoc is a township in Hastings County, Ontario, that was named in 1820 after Prince Madoc Ad Owaiin Gwynedd (say that three times fast!). Some people believe that Prince Madoc sailed from Wales to present-day Alabama in 1170—and thus was the first European to "discover" America.

Crowns on Ice

Obviously, many royals don't mind bundling up for sub-zero temperatures. They even hang out in Canada's Far North! Nunavut's **Prince Charles Island**, in northern Foxe Basin, was discovered by a Royal Canadian Air Force aerial survey in 1948. It was named after Prince Charles, who was born that same year. Nearby **Prince Regent Inlet**, a strait between Somerset Island and Baffin Island, was named by the explorer William Parry in 1819 after George Augustus Frederick. In 1811, this eldest son of George III had been appointed Prince Regent (a title given to someone who takes the throne but is too young to rule on his own). He became King George IV in 1820.

The **Prince Gustav Adolf Sea** was named—no surprise here!—after Prince Gustav Adolf, who reigned as King Gustav VI Adolf of Sweden from 1950 to 1973, and **King Christian Island** was named after King Christian IX of Denmark, who reigned from 1863 to 1906. And let's not forget Queen Victoria and her children. Divided between the Northwest Territories and Nunavut, **Victoria Island** is Canada's second-largest island (after Baffin Island). It was named in 1838 by Thomas Simpson, a trader with the Hudson's Bay Company, for Queen Victoria, who had been crowned the year before. Completing this northern royal family are **Prince Patrick Island**, named after the third son of Victoria, and **Princess Mary Lake**, named after her eldest daughter.

Boo!: Names with Ghostly or Spooky Origins

Did you imagine that ghosts lurk only in creepy attics and cemeteries and venture out just on Hallowe'en? Think again. In Canada, the spirits of the dead are out and about, popping up across the landscape, inspiring those who have experienced a close encounter to name a place or two after them!

Whooping It Up!

Many tales of ghosts seem to begin with a murder—and this one is no exception. According to legend, a man was murdered near a spring close to the Dungarvon River, which flows into the Renous River, a tributary of New Brunswick's Miramichi. From that day on, people often reported seeing the ghost of the dead man looming up after sundown. And they'd hear him too! For some reason, the vocal ghost would make a strange whooping noise whenever he appeared. Locals eventually named him the Dungarvon Whooper, and they named the spring **Whooper Spring** after his ghostly cries!

The Piper's Refrain

Can you hear the mournful pipes playing northwest of Swift Current, Newfoundland? This was the site of a bloody battle between the French and English in the 1700s, and the legend goes that ever since then, a French piper has haunted the area. **Pipers Hole River** was named after the musical ghost.

There, There

Ever heard a ghost cry? In the early 1900s, the first settlers living on the Gaspé Peninsula, east of the village of Mont-Louis, Quebec, heard moans coming from the woods. They believed that the sound wasn't simply a result of the wind blowing through the trees. They thought it was the voices of spirits. This is why their hamlet became known as **L'Anse-Pleureuse**, or "the crying village."

Can You Believe Your Eyes?

The **Haunted Lakes**, near Red Deer, Alberta, are said to get their eerie name from a Native legend. The story goes that one wintry night, two bandsmen were astonished to see an elk's head out on the ice in the middle of one of the lakes. When the men went out on the ice to retrieve it, however, it began moving away. (Creepy!) Suddenly the ice broke, and the two men were drowned. It is said that the men have haunted the lakes ever since.

Haunted Haunt

It happened in 1830. A group of Cree were sleeping peacefully by the shores of a lake. Only one man was away from the camp, out on an overnight hunting expedition. When he returned the next morning, he found to his horror that all his family and friends were dead. They had been murdered by a rival Blackfoot band!

The lone remaining Cree painted his face black in mourning and wept. But he could not rest. With revenge in his heart, he set off in pursuit of the Blackfoot—and the killing continued. For many years after this terrible event, the lake was avoided by the Cree peoples. They believed that an unusual pine tree on the shores guarded the spot of the tragedy, and that the ghosts of the murdered people haunted the area. This is how the lake, which is northeast of Calgary and is now called Pine Lake, got its original name: **Ghostpine Lake**.

Watch Out!

Imagine you are paddling your canoe down a long river on northern Vancouver Island. The water is smooth, the sun is shining, the birds are singing. Suddenly, without warning, everything changes. The water is swirling and dangerous. Your canoe is tossing and turning, and the paddle is pulled out of your grip. Next thing you know, your canoe is being sucked into the water right from under you!

What caused the canoe's spooky disappearing act? According to the Kwakwaka'wakw peoples, the culprit is a huge mythical fish-like monster called the nimpkish. This troublesome supernatural creature gave its name to both the river in which it is thought to dwell, the **Nimpkish River**, southeast of Port McNeil, and nearby **Nimpkish Lake**.

Boo to You, And Hoodoo Too

Bugaboo Creek, which flows into British Columbia's Upper Columbia River, and the **Bugaboos**, in the neighbouring Purcell Mountains, were both likely named by a Scotsman working a nearby mine. He must have been spooked by the loneliness of the place, because a bugaboo is an object of fear. A hoodoo, on the other hand, is something that brings bad luck. When Forrin Campbell was surveying some lakes northwest of Prince George, he had so many troubles, including an early freak snowstorm, that he named them the **Hoodoo Lakes**.

New Found Lande: Places Named for the Earliest Settlers

Canada's earliest settlers had to brave harsh summers and even harsher winters, struggle to clear acres of inhospitable land, and toil to produce enough food to survive. As villages and towns grew, life remained tough for the postmasters, the blacksmiths, the trappers, the traders—everyone who worked to get by in the new land. It's only fitting that some of these pioneering folk have been commemorated in the names of places from coast to coast to coast.

Early Bluenoses

Many spots in Nova Scotia were named after the first people to settle them. Capt. David Ballantyne, for instance, an early Scottish pioneer, lent his name to **Ballantynes Cove**, near the tip of Cape George, and someone named Jonathan was the inspiration for **Ben Eoin**, a community on the eastern shore of East Bay whose name is Gaelic for "Jonathan's mountain." But perhaps the most famous spot in Nova Scotia named for an early immigrant is **Peggys Cove**, the picturesque little town at the entrance to St. Margaret's Bay. It was named after Margaret Rodgers, a settler whose nickname was Peggy!

A Two-Girl Combo

When the railway was being built in the southwest corner of Saskatchewan, the engineers and surveyors stayed at a farm belonging to the McKinnon family. The town of **Vidora** was later named by these railway workers to honour their hosts. Vidora is a combination of the names of two girls: *Dora* McKinnon and her friend Vada (whose nickname was *Vi*). Two other Saskatchewan towns got their names in a similar way: **Ruthilda** (named after the two daughters, *Ruth* and *Hilda*, of the first settlers in the area) and **Baljennie** (named after Belle—although, oddly, it came out as *Bal*—and *Jennie* Ward, the first two girls born in the district).

I Want It All!

Okay, so he wasn't exactly a roughing-it-in-the-bush, tough-it-out kind of settler. Still, his is a neat story that has to be included here. The Englishman John Perceval was the second earl of Egmont, the first Baron Lovel and Holland of Enmore, and the first lord of the Admiralty. In 1763, when the Treaty of Paris ceded St. John's Island, or what is now Prince Edward Island, to the British, this confident fellow requested that the king, George III, grant him all of the territory. He planned to rule the Island from a castle like a medieval lord.

The king said no way! Nevertheless, **Cape Egmont** and **Egmont Bay**, both on the Northumberland Strait, were named for the odd earl. And Samuel Holland, who later surveyed the entire island, named **Percival Bay** after him as well. (Remember, his name was John Perceval. The bay was originally spelled with an "e," but over time, the "e" changed to an "i.") Even **Enmore** and the **Enmore River** bear the name of this greedy lord!

Strange but True

Many places in British Columbia have really strange names that owe their origins to early settlers and local heroes. **Mount Baldy Hughes**, south of Prince George, was named after—you guessed it—"Baldy" Hughes, a former stagecoach driver and trapper who lived at the base of this mountain. **Bonnevier Creek**, near Hope, was named after Charles Bonneview, a Swede who was the first homesteader in the area and a gold prospector.

Several other prospectors or people connected with the B.C. gold rushes (for more, flip to page 83) have had places named after them. **Doc English Gulch**, east of Riske Creek in the Cariboo region, was named after Benjamin Franklin "Doc" English. He arrived in the Cariboo in 1860 with a herd of cattle, which he then sold to the miners for meat. He loved trading horses—and racing them too! **Mount Shorty Stevenson**, west of Bear River, was named after an old-time prospector from New Brunswick. As you may have guessed, Shorty Stevenson was a giant of a man with a "short" nickname. And then there's **Volcanic Creek**. What do volcanoes have to do with gold-seekers? Well, Volcanic Creek and the neighbouring **Brown Creek**, north of Grand Forks, are both named for "Volcanic" Brown, a prospector who perished while searching for a "lost mine."

A Safe Haven

The community of **Brainard**, west of Grande Prairie, Alberta, was named after Lee Brainard. He came with his family to the Richdale area from Montana in 1906, bringing with him seven hundred cattle and one hundred horses. But the very first winter was extremely harsh: all the animals on Brainard's ranch died. And that's not all. There was a devastating blizzard that killed Brainard's son and one of the hired hands. Brainard himself barely managed to find his way to a neighbour's ranch in the storm. Scarred by these experiences, he went back to Montana for a time, but soon he returned again to Alberta, to the Hythe area. Here he turned to farming once more, and this time he was a great success. To the end of his days, however, in memory of his son and his ranch hand, he kept his window blinds open at night. He wanted to be sure that, in darkness or storms, travellers could be guided to safety.

By and By

The Saskatchewan pioneer Brooks Partidge was asked to move his shack so the railway could pass over that spot. It had to get "by," he was told. He did as he was asked, and as a result, the hamlet that grew up on his land was named **Brooksby**! Another settler refused to give up his land when the Canadian Pacific Railway wanted to build there. Instead, he chose to "hold fast." The railway ended up revising the route and bypassing the disputed land. The nearby village north of Regina, which eventually grew into a town, became known as **Holdfast**.

Croque Monsieur

New Brunswick's **Crocks Point**, west of Fredericton, was likely named for an early settler—or at least for his nickname. Apparently, Jean Cyr had a sugar bush and was known for the many maple sugar products he made. People were always asking him, "Do you have something to munch?" But in French, the word for "munch" is *croquer*. Over the years, English-speakers also began using the word *croquer* when they spoke to Cyr, but they changed it slightly to "crock." Soon everyone was using that word to refer to Jean Cyr himself! And after a time, the place where he lived became known as Crocks Point.

From Jens to John

The only inland seaport in Canada, **Churchill**, Manitoba, is on the west coast of Hudson Bay, at the mouth of the **Churchill River**. The river was originally known as the Missinipi by the local Native peoples, but it was renamed by English settlers for John Churchill, a governor of the Hudson's Bay Company in the late 1600s. The port at that site was originally called Munk's Harbour, after Capt. Jens Munk. This Norwegian explorer probably arrived there in 1619 while searching for the Northwest Passage. He and his sixty-four crew members wintered at the site, but tragically, all but three died of scurvy. Then, in 1717, a permanent Hudson's Bay Company fur-trading post was built near the mouth of the Churchill River. It was called Churchill only briefly, and then it became known as Prince of Wales's Fort. When it was rebuilt upstream in 1783, it kept both names, but the town that eventually replaced the post took the name Churchill.

Something to Crow About

In Nova Scotia, there were many early Scottish settlers with the name John Macdonald—but there was only one with a falling-down farm and a flock of crows always overhead. He was known as Johnnie "Crowbush" Macdonald, and **Crowbush Cove**, on the Gulf of the St. Lawrence, is named after him.

Local Name-Dropping

In Ontario, many places were named for important local citizens. Postmasters lent their names to several towns, including **Harwood**, **Huntsville**, **Janetville**, **Klueys Bay**, **Lefaivre**, **Maxwell**, **Morton**, and **Schutt**. There are also places named after blacksmiths (**Harrisburg**), shoemakers (**Fisherville**), lawyers (**Gurd**), and judges (**Hagarty**). Some places, such as **Ignace**, were named for the Native Canadians who guided the early settlers. **Kingsville**, just west of Leamington, was named after the first person to build a house in the community. And **Haley Station**, north of Renfrew, was named for George Haley, a local farmer who, in 1878, gave the Canadian Pacific Railway the right-of-way through his farm.

Some Ontario places flip-flopped on their names. A village on the Bay of Quinte was first named Mill Point (because of its sawmill), then it changed to Bowen (after the first postmaster), and then it changed back to Mill Point again. In 1881, it was finally named **Desoronto** after John Deserontyon, the Mohawk chief who had first settled the village in 1784.

Making Their **Mark**: Names from **Black History**

Some blacks came here as early as the late eighteenth century, having fought with the British against the Americans during the Revolutionary War. In the nineteenth century, blacks made their way to freedom in Canada along the Underground Railroad. And today they come from all over the world. All across this nation, there are place names honouring the important role black Canadians have played in our history.

Black Nova Scotians

The province with perhaps the most enduring tradition of black settlement is Nova Scotia. The vast majority of those blacks who came in the wake of the American Revolution settled there, and they were joined in the next century by "passengers" from the Underground Railroad (look across the page to learn more). Soon, blacks made up a higher percentage of the population in Nova Scotia than in any other province in Canada. (Today only Ontario surpasses Nova Scotia in this respect.)

By the late 1700s, most of Nova Scotia's largest towns had sizeable all-black settlements nearby. Many local place names reflect that significant black presence. **Isaacs Harbour**, for instance, which lies east of Country Harbour, was named for Isaac Webb, one of the many black Loyalists who came to the area in 1783. Halifax's black community, meanwhile, eventually came to be called **Africville**, a name possibly chosen by local whites. In one of the most controversial chapters of black history in Nova Scotia, the land on which Africville sat was acquired by the city in the 1960s. The residents were forced to leave and the settlement was destroyed. In 2002, however, the original location of the village was designated a National Historic Site.

Ride 'Em, Cowboy

John Ware was born in the southern United States, probably into slavery. When the Civil War brought an end to slavery, Ware headed to Texas and became a cowboy. Then he decided to settle in the Canadian West. He arrived in Alberta in 1882 and began working for local ranchers. Soon he was ranching for himself on the Red Deer River. He quickly became a famous pioneer cowboy. Although he died in 1905 after a fall from a horse, his name lives on. Three landmarks near present-day Calgary were named after him: **Mount Ware**, **Ware Creek**, and **John Ware Ridge**.

North to Freedom

Though some Loyalists did bring slaves with them from New England in the late 1700s, slavery never really got much of a foothold in Canada. In 1833, the institution was formally outlawed in all British North American colonies by an act of the English Parliament. In the United States, however, slavery continued, and many of those who wanted to escape from it began to look to Canada as a place of safety and freedom. Soon, a secret, illegal network had been established. Called the Underground Railroad, this was an organization of people who helped fugitive slaves reach, and then cross, the border. In all, the Underground Railroad helped to bring about thirty thousand blacks to Canada.

Many of the blacks who escaped this way settled in Ontario, and their stories are reflected in several of the province's place names. **Dawn**, the name given to a township in Lambton County in 1829, perhaps commemorates the "dawn" of freedom for the fugitive blacks who had arrived there the year before. Wilberforce, which lies northwest of London and has since been renamed **Lucan**, was named in the 1930s to honour William Wilberforce, an Englishman who fought against slavery. From 1829 to the mid-1840s, many fugitive slaves settled in Wilberforce. **Shanty Bay**, northeast of Barrie, was, like Wilberforce, also first settled by blacks. When they arrived in 1831, many built shanties (shacks) as their first shelters.

A few places were even named after individual settlers. The town of **Mitchell**, on the North Thames River, was named in 1847 by the local postmaster for the black man who had first settled the town and provided lodgings for travellers in the 1830s. Some say that **Priceville**, east of Durham, also has a connection to the Underground Railroad, having been named either for a "conductor" who helped fugitive slaves or for the black settler who first surveyed the community.

Doing the Can-can

Deas Island, at the mouth of the Fraser River in British Columbia, was named after John Deas. His parents had been slaves in South Carolina, but John wanted a life of freedom and so headed north for Victoria. Around 1861, he began making tin cans for a local salmon fishery. When the owner died, Deas took over as foreman. It was a multicultural affair. The fish were provided by local Native peoples, Chinese immigrants were employed as labourers, and Deas, a black man, ran the show. Soon Deas's diverse enterprise was exporting thousands of cans of salmon to Britain every year!

This or That?: Names of Change and Controversy

Just because you name a place, that doesn't mean the name will stick. There are all kinds of reasons that place names change—history, politics, religion, or simple convenience. Read on for some examples of Canadian place name flip-flops!

Devils, Devils Everywhere!

Watch out! Has the Devil been to Newfoundland? Maybe he's been whooping it up at **Devils Dancing Table**, a hill on the western shore of North Bay. If you can't find him there, try looking at **Devils Dressing Table**, a marsh on the Avalon Peninsula, or at **Devils Dining Table**, a steep cliff on Henley Island. Or maybe he's climbing the **Devils Stairway**, a rock formation at Cape Broyle. (Some say his footprints can be seen in the cliff-face.) You certainly won't find him at Devil's Cove, northeast of Carbonear. The inhabitants of the area had the name changed in 1812 because they believed it to be "barbarous, execrable, and impious." The cove is now called **Jobs Cove**, in honour of either a local family or the long-suffering Job from the Bible.

The Winds of War

During the First World War, anti-German sentiment was running high, and that resulted in several places doing name flip-flops. **Kitchener**, Ontario, was one. Originally settled by German Mennonites in the nineteenth century, the town changed its name from Berlin in 1916 to commemorate Lord Horatio Kitchener, the British secretary of war. He was killed that same year when the ship in which he was travelling struck a German mine and sank.

Similar anti-German feelings caused the townspeople of Dusseldorf, Alberta, to change its name to **Freedom** in 1919.

Don't Rename It!

Mount Logan, the highest peak in Canada and the second tallest mountain in North America, lies near the Yukon-Alaska border. It was named after Sir William Edmond Logan, a geologist who founded the Geological Survey of Canada in 1842 and played a major role in the mapping of our country. There can't be any controversy about that, right? Wrong!

Within days of the September 2000 death of Pierre Elliott Trudeau, one of Canada's longest-serving prime ministers, the government announced that it would rename Mount Logan after him. Trudeau was an avid outdoorsman who had once planned to climb the mountain, and this was thought to be a fitting tribute. But the proposed name change sparked great debate across the nation, especially among geographers, who objected to the idea of one of Canada's greatest surveyors being erased from the map. The government eventually backed down—and Mount Logan's name remains untouched.

The Peak of His Career

Castle Mountain, northwest of Banff, was named in 1858 by Dr. James Hector. He thought the prominent mountain with its 2,722-metre (8,930-foot) peak looked like a fortress with parapets. But in 1946, Canada's prime minister, William Lyon Mackenzie King, decided to change the name of the mountain. The Second World War was raging, and King wanted to honour Gen. Dwight D. Eisenhower, the supreme commander of the Allied forces in Europe. Castle Mountain became Mount Eisenhower.

Oops! It wasn't a popular decision. After many years of public outcry, petitions, and appeals, the governments of Canada and Alberta were finally convinced to restore the mountain's original name in 1979. But Eisenhower wasn't forgotten. The mountain's most prominent (but not its highest) peak was named **Eisenhower Peak**.

Bishop's Request

A small community in northwestern Alberta was originally known as Rahab, but that was also the name of a scandalous woman from the Bible. In 1937 the bishop complained, and so the town's name was changed. How was the new name picked? Three officials of the Northern Alberta Railways helped out. The first two letters in their last names (Collins, Deakins, and Saunders) were put together to create **Codesa**.

O Canada!: Places Named for Great Canadians

Like most countries, Canada likes to honour its most accomplished citizens. Spread across this land, you'll find places named for Nobel Prize winners, composers, long-distance runners and walkers—and even an Indian impostor!

In Your Name ...

William Cormack was an explorer and a naturalist. He was born in St. John's, Newfoundland, in 1786, but he went to Scotland to study. In 1822, he returned to his native island to run the family business. And during his very first autumn back home, he crossed Newfoundland on foot from coast to coast! Twice, Cormack also travelled into the interior of the island to find out about its geography and learn more about the Native Beothuk peoples. Shawnandithit, the last surviving Beothuk, even lived in his home for several years. (**Shanadithit Brook**, which flows into Red Indian Lake, is named after her, though it's spelled differently.) For a few years before Shawnandithit died, Cormack made many attempts to locate other members of her band, but he was unsuccessful. When she died in 1829, her people died with her. The community of **Cormack**, north of Deer Lake, was eventually named for William Cormack, as were **Lake Cormack**, **Mount Cormack**, and the **Cormack Trail**, a 182-kilometre (113-mile) coastal hike from Petites, on the south coast of the island, to St. George's, on the west coast.

Banting Lake, south of Musgrave Harbour, is another Newfoundland spot named after an important Canadian. Sir Frederick Banting was the co-discoverer of insulin, a life-saving therapy for those with diabetes. He and one of his colleagues, J. J. R. Macleod, won the Nobel Prize for Medicine in 1923.

Just Bones

Joseph Tyrrell was a scientist and an explorer of northwestern Canada. In 1893, accompanied by his brother, James Tyrrell, he surveyed the land between Lake Athabasca and Chesterfield Inlet. **Mount Tyrrell** is named after one or both of these men.

When Tyrrell was surveying the badlands of Alberta, he came face to face with a skull. (Must have been a shock!) It turned out to be a dinosaur fossil, only the first of many he would find in the area. That's why Drumheller's Royal Tyrrell Museum of Palaeontology, which is visited by people from all over the world, is also named after him.

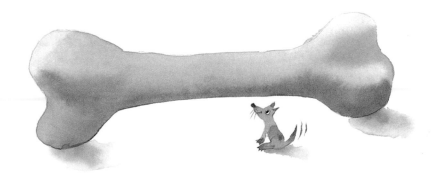

Hogan's a Hero

The **Hogan Trail**, a hiking trail that begins in Hawke's Bay, Newfoundland, was named for John Hogan. He was a member of the Newfoundland Rangers, a police force that patrolled the island's outports and other isolated communities in the 1930s and 1940s.

In May 1943, Hogan was on a Royal Canadian Air Force flight to Gander when the plane suddenly filled with smoke. All the occupants bailed out by parachute, but they became separated on the way down. Hogan landed safely, but he had no way of knowing what had happened to the other passengers. After spending a night camping under his parachute, he determined which direction he needed to go and started walking for the coast, hoping to find a settlement along the way. He hadn't gone far when he came across Corporal Butt, another of the plane's passengers. The corporal hadn't been so lucky—in fact, because he had landed in water, his feet were frozen and he was unable to walk on his own. Hogan helped the corporal make it to a hunting cabin three days away, but that was as far as Butt could go.

Still, Hogan stuck with him. They had no food or equipment, and no idea if any rescuers were looking for them. But Hogan kept them both alive, trapping rabbits and making tea from spruce needles to keep them nourished. After fifty-two days, they were at last spotted by a survey team that just happened to be crossing a nearby pond. Yet even after his long ordeal, the tenacious Hogan insisted on walking the rest of the way back to civilization under his own steam.

Why Not, Indeed!

The mountains in British Columbia's **Liberated Group**, which include **Agnes Macphail, Nellie McClung,** and **Charlotte Whitton**, are named after several activists famous for their work in the women's liberation movement. Nearby **Why Not Mountain** is named for the motto of that movement.

National Notes

Calixa Lavallée was born in 1842 near Verchères, Canada East (which is now known as Quebec). His father gave him music lessons, and by the time he was thirteen, he had made his first appearance as a concert pianist. Twice, Lavallée moved to the United States to live, and he even fought in the American Civil War. After returning to Montreal in 1873 to set up a music studio with some friends, Lavallée was able to finance a trip to Paris to study. When he returned to Montreal again, the now famous pianist, organist, teacher, and composer was commissioned to write a piece of music for a national convention of French Canadians. (The French lyrics were written by Adolphe-Basile Routhier.) The piece was first performed publicly at an ice rink in Quebec City in 1880. In 1908, English words to the piece (that's right, they are *not* a translation of the French) were written by an Ontario schoolteacher, Robert Stanley Weir, and over the years, the song became very popular in Canada. Have you guessed what it is yet? In 1980, one hundred years after it was first written, the song became Canada's national anthem, "O Canada." A region in Champlain County, Quebec, was named **Lavallée** in honour of the anthem's composer.

Passing the Time of Day

The Canadian Pacific Railway might not have made it to the Rockies without Sir Sandford Fleming. In 1871, he was appointed engineer-in-chief of the railway, and he surveyed the route from Fort William to the Rockies and through two passes, Kicking Horse Pass and Yellowhead.

At the time, every community in the country—and indeed in the world!—set its clock according to local astronomical conditions. Fleming realized that a transcontinental railway needed to run on a twenty-four-hour time system that everyone could rely on. He created what we now call standard time by using lines of longitude to divide the earth into twenty-four time zones. Once these time zones had been established, everyone in Canada could figure out the exact time anywhere from coast to coast to coast.

There are many places named after the guy with the watch in his hand. The **Sir Sandford Fleming Range** of mountains are north of Rogers Pass, B.C. **Fleming Island** and **Sandford Island** are both in Barkley Sound, also in B.C. And there is even a town named **Fleming** in Saskatchewan, just west of the Manitoba border, on (naturally!) the Canadian Pacific Railway line between Winnipeg and Regina.

Got Get-up and Go!

Grey Owl Lake, in Ontario's Algonquin Park, is named after Archibald Belaney, also known as Grey Owl. As a child, this Englishman dreamed of being a Native Canadian. He immigrated to northern Canada in 1905 and began telling people that one parent was Scottish and the other Apache, making him half-Native. Using the name Grey Owl, he started to write popular stories of his experiences living in the wilderness with the Ojibwa. His Iroquois wife, Anahareo, introduced him to the importance of wilderness and animal conservation, and he eventually became a notable spokesperson for this issue. That he was not in fact Native *at all* was not uncovered until after his death in 1938.

Henry of the Mounties

After Roald Amundsen successfully navigated the Northwest Passage in 1906, no one else tried again until the 1940s. Then Henry Asbjorn Larsen, commanding the RCMP patrol vessel *St. Roch*, made the trip. It was the first time the passage had been crossed from east to west. Larsen also later completed the voyage in just one season. In 1965, the body of water surrounded by Boothia Peninsula and the Victoria, King William, and Prince of Wales islands was named **Larsen Sound** in his honour.

Not from Around Here: Places Named for **Amazing Non-Canadians**

You certainly don't have to be a Canadian to have a place in Canada named after you. In fact, there are places in this country named for a Greek explorer, a Japanese general, and an English nurse or two. Why, there's even a gulf named after the first person, a Norwegian, ever to travel through the Northwest Passage. And that's not all …

Mapping the World—and Newfoundland

Capt. James Cook was the greatest navigator of his time. He actually sailed around the world twice! And during his decades of exploration, Cook charted parts of New Zealand and Australia, investigated the Antarctic Ocean, and explored what we now call Vanuatu and Hawaii. In the 1750s and 1760s, he also charted part of the Gaspé Peninsula and all of Newfoundland's dangerous coast, including St. John's harbour. It's no surprise, then, that so many places on the island are named for him. You can visit **Cook's Lookout**, which is on the south coast, near Burin, and two different places named **Cook's Cove**, one in Humber Arm and one in Trinity Bay. **Cook's Harbour**, on the Strait of Belle Isle, is also named after this extraordinary Englishman.

The Guy with the Apple, Right?

It used to be called Millbank Station, but in 1881, this community north of Stratford, Ontario, was renamed **Newton**, in honour of the great British scientist Sir Isaac Newton, the first person to understand the force of gravity.

In Time of War

In 1904–05, there was a war raging between Russia and Japan. A Japanese general named Kuroki passed through Saskatchewan on his way to the United States to ask for financial assistance for his country. The Canadian National Railway, which was at the time building in the district through which the general travelled, named the town of **Kuroki**, Saskatchewan, after him.

Nurses Extraordinaire

Originally called Buttermilk Creek, a small community on the St. John River, north of Hartland, New Brunswick, was renamed **Florenceville** in 1855. This new name was a tribute to Florence Nightingale, who had the previous year tirelessly nursed wounded soldiers during the Crimean War, a conflict between Russia and the Ottoman Empire (with England and France). At this time, there were no nurses as we know them today, and family members usually tended their sick at home. After the war, Nightingale started a training school in her hometown of London, England, so would-be nurses could learn how to care for those in need. Today she is considered the founder of modern nursing.

The hamlet of **Cavell**, Saskatchewan, was also named for an English nurse. Edith Cavell was working at a hospital in Brussels, Belgium, during the First World War. When the Germans occupied the city in 1915, she helped many Allied soldiers escape to and cross the Dutch border. When her activities were discovered by the Germans, she was arrested and executed. This brave and selfless woman is also remembered in a **Mount Edith Cavell** near Jasper, Alberta.

A Record-breaker

Like James Cook, the British explorer Sir William Edward Parry ranks among the great navigators of the world. He made five Arctic expeditions and contributed much of the knowledge that led to the eventual discovery of the Northwest Passage and the North Pole. A record-breaker himself, Parry in 1827 travelled as far north as 82°45'N, a mark that stood for forty-nine years! He also had a lot to do with naming many geographic features in Canada's North.

What's named after Parry himself? **Parry Channel**, a sea passage running from east to west through the Arctic islands, and the **Parry Islands**, a group of High Arctic islands (including Melville, Bathurst, and Cornwallis) that he discovered in 1819.

Hold on to Your Hat!

In 1826, Sir John Franklin, who was eventually lost looking for the Northwest Passage, gave the name **Beaufort Sea** to the part of the Arctic Ocean that is west of the Banks and Prince Patrick islands in the Northwest Territories and north of Yukon. Sir Francis Beaufort was at that time the hydrographer to the British Admiralty—that is, the man in charge of surveying and charting bodies of water. Beaufort was also the inventor of the Beaufort scale, which ranks wind speed. By observing the way things react in different wind velocities, you can place them on Beaufort's scale and measure their force. For example, 0 is calm (smoke rises straight up into the air), 2 is a light breeze (leaves rustle and you can feel wind on your face), 5 is a fresh breeze (small leafy trees sway), 9 is a strong gale (slight structural damage can occur), and 12 is hurricane force (winds of more than 118 kilometres, or 73 miles, an hour).

Through the Passage

When the Norwegian explorer Roald Amundsen arrived in the Arctic in August 1903, he, like so many men before him, was looking for the Northwest Passage. Amundsen didn't get very far before he realized that winter was fast approaching and he needed a safe place for his ship and crew to ride out the harsh months ahead. When he happened upon a deep, narrow inlet with no pack ice in sight, he knew it was the perfect place to harbour his wooden ship, the *Gjoa*. Amundsen called this spot on King William Island "the finest little harbour in the world," and he named it **Gjoa Haven**, after his ship. It took two more years (and another two tough winters!), but in 1906, Amundsen did become the first man to make it through the long-sought Northwest Passage. A few years later, the British Admiralty named an area of the Beaufort Sea (between the islands of Victoria and Banks and the north shore of the Northwest Territories mainland) **Amundsen Gulf** in his honour.

Did He or Didn't He?

The **Strait of Juan de Fuca** was named after a Greek explorer who might have sailed through those waters while searching for the Northwest Passage in 1592. The story of his journey was published in 1625, but some people doubt he ever really made it there. When Capt. Charles Barkley sailed to Vancouver Island in 1787 and found the opening in the coast to be exactly as Fuca had described it, however, he named the strait after him.

Oops! My Mistake

Dionisio Alcalá Galiano, the captain of the Spanish ship *Sutil*, was exploring British Columbia's Gulf Islands in 1792. When he sailed into one bay west of White Rock, he thought there was a passage at its end. He was wrong, so he named the bay Ensenada del Engaño, which is Spanish for "mistake bay." It was later renamed **Boundary Bay** because it is intersected by the international boundary that runs between British Columbia and Washington State. **Galiano Island**, which lies just southwest of Boundary Bay, was named after Captain Galiano.

That same year, Galiano named **Hernando Island** and **Cortes Island**, south and east of Quadra Island, respectively, after Hernando Cortes, the conqueror of Mexico. He also named **Valdes Island**, north of Galiano Island, after Cayetano Valdés y Vazan, the captain of the Spanish ship *Mexicana*. This eighteenth-century mariner accompanied Galiano on his exploration of the area between Vancouver Island and the mainland.

George Vancouver, the famous English explorer, met the two Spanish ships and their captains off Point Grey (now a suburb of Vancouver) on June 22, 1792, and in memory of this occasion, he called the place **Spanish Bank**. To commemorate the same meeting, a bay near Vancouver was named **English Bay**.

Chill Out

The **Agassiz Ice Cap**, on Ellesmere Island, and Manitoba's glacial **Lake Agassiz** are both named after Louis Agassiz, an extraordinary Swiss-American scientist and professor. Agassiz was one of the first to suggest (and present proof) that glaciers once covered huge parts of the globe.

Murder, Mayhem, and
Missing Men: Names of Notoriety

One way to get a place named after you is to be kind, decent, honest, upstanding, and good. Another way is … well, to be really, really bad! Not convinced? Read up on these pirates, counterfeiters, bootleggers, and thieves. You'll find all these notorious scoundrels immortalized in Canada's place names.

Avast, Ye Landlubbers!

Where there is water and ships, there were once pirates. Newfoundland was no exception, and many of the names along the coast reflect the influence of these dastardly seafarers. **Black Joke Cove**, on the northern shore of Belle Isle, is named after the *Black Joke*. One of the most notorious pirate ships, the *Black Joke* would hide in this hard-to-spot cove and then swoop down on merchant ships and plunder them for riches and valuable goods.

The community now known as **Marysvale** was earlier known as Turkish Gut. That's because the pirates who menaced Newfoundland in the seventeenth century came from Turkey. And "gut"? That's a term for a channel of water.

St. Chad's, northwest of Eastport, was originally called Damnable Harbour. The story goes that pirates were hiding in the harbour behind a small island, trying to avoid detection by sailors of the Royal Navy, who were hot in pursuit. But when a member of the pirate crew bumped into the ship's bell, the noise was loud enough that the navy sailors heard it and came to investigate. The pirates were caught all because of the "damnable bell"!

Hide and Seek

Nova Scotia had its share of pirates too. One bay southwest of Chester was a perfect place for them because it contained 365 islands. Just think of all the places to hide! One of its early names was Baye de Toutes Iles, or "bay of many islands." Now it is known as **Mahone Bay**, since *mahonne* is the French name of a particular kind of pirate ship.

Crime Doesn't Pay

A band of Crow warriors were in Blackfoot territory on a horse-stealing mission when they were forced to camp overnight in a mountain pass on the Alberta–B.C. border. That night, a party of angry Blackfoot surprised the trespassers in their "nest" and killed them. Ever since, the place has been called **Crowsnest Pass**.

Island Mysteries

Okay, the name **Oak Island** isn't that interesting. Probably there were simply lots of oak trees on it at one time. But what is interesting is what else may be on this Nova Scotia island. Countless stories claim that treasure was buried here centuries ago. A wooden shaft and several subterranean oak platforms were first discovered on the island in 1795. Many people have tried to dig down to find the buried wealth they're convinced is there, but whenever a certain depth is reached, water rushes into the pit, foiling their efforts. The secret remains unsolved to this day.

Who built the pit? No one knows, but legend has it that the bosses hauled the poor workers who did the digging over to a nearby island, off Pinkeys Point, and killed them there to ensure that the location of the treasure pit would remain a secret. Human remains have been found on this island. It's no wonder it was given the creepy name **Murder Island**.

Secret Shipments

Nova Scotia even had pirates of a different sort, and one small cove, originally called Anse-aux-Hirondelles, or "swallow cove," because of the many swallows that nested on its high cliffs, now has a name to reflect that.

In 1919, an amendment to the American Constitution prohibited by law the manufacture and sale of any alcoholic drink in the United States. This didn't apply in Nova Scotia, of course, and soon "rum runners" from the southwestern parts of the province were loading boats with alcohol in the dead of night and sailing across the waters to the nearby American coast, where they would secretly and illegally sell liquor to lots of thirsty Americans. One of the places from which the alcohol was transported was this secluded cove south of Meteghan. That's how it got its final name—**Smuggler's Cove**!

Tragedy!

Two places in Manitoba were named after a tragic event that occurred in 1736. That year, a party of Sioux warriors killed a missionary named Father Aulneau and twenty of his companions on an island in the Lake of the Woods. The island became known as **Massacre Island**, and the hamlet that grew up nearby, northeast of Emerson, became known as **Arnaud**, after Father Aulneau (albeit slightly misspelled).

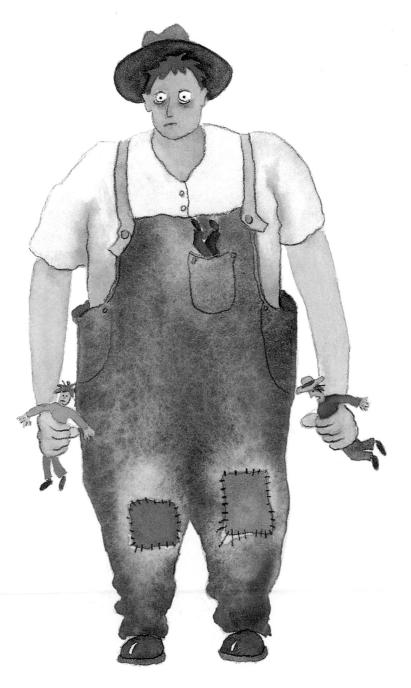

Making Bones about It

The Canadian Pacific Railway founded the town of **Indian Head**, east of Regina, in 1882. How did the town get its unusual name? One story claims that when the railway survey team was working near the site of the station, they found the skull of a Native person and decided to name the town after this gruesome find!

Notorious Albertans

Bertha Ekelund was quite a gal! She was a known counterfeiter who was jailed for passing fake money. But the oldtimers in her area were quite fond of her, and so a creek, a lake, and a 2,400-metre (8,000-foot) peak in the southwest corner of the province were all named after her. Yup, that'd be **Bertha Creek**, **Bertha Lake**, and **Bertha Peak**!

Big Jim Creek, which flows into Willow Creek in the southwestern corner of the province, was likely named after Big Jim McDonough. This tough guy came to the area in 1884. He was a rancher with an attitude. When three men in his employ vanished mysteriously, there was great suspicion that he had done them in. But Big Jim was never arrested or put on trial, and he died a free man in 1898. When the new owner of his ranch house found a big box of quicklime up in his attic, no one assumed that it had been purchased for its most common use, whitewashing or painting. Nope, suspicious minds immediately jumped to the conclusion that Big Jim had used the quicklime to poison the missing men!

Gadsby Lake, east of Red Deer, was named after James Gadsby. When he was a young man, Gadsby moved to the United States, where it is believed he joined up with Jesse James's infamous frontier gang. After years of lawlessness down south, Gadsby returned to Canada for more of the same. He was involved in importing liquor near Calgary, and the North-West Mounted Police were constantly trying to hunt him down. They were unsuccessful, though. Like Big Jim McDonough, he died a free man, in 1932.

Red Rapids

At the mouth of the Coppermine River, in the Northwest Territories, a trading post was established in 1916. First known as Coronation, after the gulf on which it was situated, the hamlet was renamed Coppermine in 1930, after the river. But in 1996, its name was changed to **Kugluktuk**. *Kugluktuk* is an Inuktitut word meaning "place of rapids." The name likely refers to the nearby **Bloody Falls**, which were given their grisly name by the explorer Samuel Hearne in 1771. The story goes that Hearne and his travelling companions, a group of Chipewyan warriors, came across a group of Inuit near the falls—and the Chipewyans killed them all. Today Bloody Falls is recognized as a National Historic Site.

Jemmy Jones and the Jenny Jones

Capt. James "Jemmy" Jones had many exploits. In 1865, he was at last put in jail in Victoria because he hadn't paid his debts. Unfortunately for him, his schooner, the *Jenny Jones*, was abandoned in an Oregon harbour. Seized by an American marshal, the schooner was going to be taken to Seattle and sold. Jones couldn't let that happen, so he escaped from jail, went to Oregon, disguised himself as a woman, boarded his ship, and went along as a passenger as the marshal sailed her to Seattle. When the marshal went ashore for a break one evening, Jones took the opportunity to sail away—to Mexico! Sometime later he was arrested again, this time for stealing his own ship. But the charges were dropped when he explained that the marshal had left the ship, not the other way around. **Jemmy Jones Island** in B.C.'s Oak Bay, the spot where Jones once sank a different schooner, is named after the notorious captain.

More Deadmen

The ship of the explorer James Knight and his crew got locked into the ice near Marble Island, in today's Nunavut, while they were searching for the Northwest Passage. All the men eventually died of cold and starvation. Marble Island and nearby **Deadman's Island**, which gets its name from the tragedy, contain the victims' graves and even some belongings they left behind.

Lest We Forget: Places Named for Significant Events

Wars, battles, gold rushes, a search for a lost explorer—these events are just a few of those that have dramatically touched the lives of Canadians. This country is dotted with place names that are permanent reminders of these moments in history—and the courage, fear, hope, and persistence of those who lived through them.

War Stories

Canadian soldiers have a long and proud history of distinguishing themselves in war, and there are several place names in Canada that honour these brave people. A community on the eastern boundary of Moncton, New Brunswick, was renamed **Dieppe** in 1946 to commemorate the thousands of Canadians who fought and died in a raid on the French port of the same name. More than nine hundred Canadian soldiers were killed during this disastrous single-day battle of the Second World War.

The **Battle of Britain Range**, south of Muncho Lake Provincial Park in northern British Columbia, commemorates a 1940 clash in the sky, when the German air attack on Britain was successfully repelled by the British air force. Within the range are **Mount Churchill** and **Mount Roosevelt**, named for the two key Allied leaders, Sir Winston Churchill and Franklin Delano Roosevelt. **Yalta Peak** and **Teheran Mountain** remember two of the cities where these men met to plan Allied strategy for the war. There are also mountains named for some of the most famous Second World War battles in which Canadians served, including **Dieppe Mountain**, **Falaise Mountain**, and **Ortona Mountain**.

But not all place names that recall wars necessarily had Canadian participants. A community east of Cambridge-Narrows, New Brunswick, was named **Waterloo Corner** in honour of the Battle of Waterloo. This was the famous victory of Britain's Duke of Wellington over Napoleon on June 18, 1815. The Ontario city of **Waterloo** was also named to mark this decisive achievement.

The Last Spike

When the Canadian Pacific Railway finally reached its end, west of Revelstoke, B.C., there was a ceremony to drive in the last spike. Donald A. Smith, one of the men who financed the venture, had the honour of hammering it home on November 7, 1885. Canada was finally linked from sea to sea!

Everyone agreed that the site of such a significant event needed a grand name. William Van Horne, the general manager of the CPR, also wanted something that would honour Smith and the other financial backers, so he chose **Craigellachie**. What does this unusual name have to do with money or railways? Well, it is actually the name of a massive rock near Banffshire, Scotland, where Smith and his cousin George Stephen had grown up. When Stephen learned that they had got the last-minute funds they needed to finish the CPR, he let Smith know through a telegraph that simply read, "Stand fast, Craigellachie!" a reference to the local clan's rallying cry. When Van Horne learned of this story, he knew he had found the perfect name for the site of the last spike.

A Famous Foe

Some battles have been fought on our own soil, and **Cut Knife Hill**, west of Battleford, Saskatchewan, was named for just such an event. One day in the late nineteenth century, a small party of Sarcee hunters stopped on this hill to scout for buffalo. Suddenly they were surrounded by a band of enemy Cree. The Cree sent for the rest of their band members and their chief to come and watch the fighting. When the Cree chief arrived, he realized that Cut Knife, the Sarcee chief, was among the small group. Cut Knife was famous for his strength and his abilities as a fighter. Knowing this, the Cree chief bravely ordered his people not to use any guns; he wanted to beat Cut Knife at his own game, using only hand-to-hand fighting. When the Sarcees were eventually defeated, the proud Cree victors named the spot Cut Knife Hill after their conquered enemy.

What a Rush!

In 1857, miners who had had little luck panning for gold in California decided to look north to the Fraser River in British Columbia. When they stopped on a sandbar in the river, they discovered some golden nuggets. News got out, and the Fraser River Gold Rush was on!

Many places in British Columbia were soon being named after the people who came to prospect for gold during this rush and the Cariboo Gold Rush of the early 1860s. Other spots were named for events that took place during this time of both broken dreams and incredible good fortune.

Ahbau Lake, northeast of Quesnel, was named after an old Chinese trader who lived on this lake and prospected nearby. **Barkerville**, east of Quesnel, was named after Billy Barker. This sailor heard about the Fraser River Gold Rush and came ashore here in 1858. Four years later, the stocky man with the black bushy beard was still digging for gold in the region. He was almost ready to give up when he dug a little deeper and struck it rich! Many others weren't so lucky. **Deception Creek**, which flows into Mahood Lake, got its name because miners there believed they would find huge gold deposits—but never did.

Bonanza!

Of course, the rushes in the Fraser River and Cariboo Mountains weren't Canada's only gold rushes. In 1896, three men were out moose hunting in the Yukon. George Washington Carmack, "Skookum" Jim Mason, and "Tagish" Charley made their camp on Rabbit Creek, a small tributary of the Klondike River, about five kilometres (three miles) from Dawson. The men had heard stories from prospectors about gold, but they thought it was a waste of time looking for it. On this day, however, one of the men was washing a pan in the water of Rabbit Creek when he suddenly saw a golden glimmer on the bottom. Imagine his excitement when he reached down into the water and pulled out a nugget of gold! He had struck gold without even trying. Carmack knew that the Spanish word for a source of wealth was *bonanza*. He renamed the creek **Bonanza Creek** in celebration of the lucky find—and the Klondike Gold Rush was born!

Naming the Klondike

News of the find at Bonanza Creek spread like wildfire. By 1898, professional prospectors were pouring into the area from Canada, the U.S., and even the goldfields of Australia and South Africa. Tens of thousands arrived at what would turn out to be the biggest strike of all—the Klondike! And as they moved through Canada's North seeking gold, they left a trail of new place names in their wake.

Many creeks were named by the hopeful miners who panned them for gold. There was **Gold Bottom** and—if you can believe it—**Too Much Gold Creek**! **Hunker Creek** was named after Andrew Hunker, the prospector who discovered gold in it in 1896. **Eldorado Creek**, a tributary of Bonanza Creek, was also given a Spanish name when it was discovered to be one of the richest gold streams in the world. El Dorado is the name of a legendary South American city of gold, wealth, and opportunity.

Miners also searched the hills around Bonanza Creek for gold. Their theory was that some local streams could have changed course over the years, leaving gold behind in the surrounding hills. Not everyone bought this theory, however, which is how one hill came to be named **Cheechako Hill**. *Cheechako* is a Native word meaning "greenhorn." The old hands believed that only a naive *cheechako* would look for gold on a hill, but the greenhorns had the last laugh—it turned out the hills *were* full of gold. One of them was even given the name **Gold Hill**!

Faro, a town in the Pelly River valley, was named after the first claim staked in the area. It, in turn, was named after a card game popular with miners who enjoyed gambling. **Carmacks**, a village on the west bank of the Yukon River, was named in 1908 for strike-it-rich, start-the-rush George Washington Carmack. He'd developed local coal deposits and begun operating a trading post at this place fifteen years earlier.

Looking for Franklin

One of the most extended adventure stories to take place on Canadian soil was the search for the Northwest Passage. Countless place names throughout the North commemorate the men—from Martin Frobisher to Henry Hudson to Roald Amundsen—who, over three centuries, searched for this mythical route to the riches of the Far East.

But perhaps the most famous Arctic explorer was John Franklin, who went missing in 1845 while trying to find the passage. Over the next several years, there were wide-ranging searches for the members of the lost Franklin expedition. In all, thirty-two campaigns set out to find them. All this activity in the North revealed little about the fate of Franklin and his crew, but it did finally complete the map of the Canadian Arctic and add many more place names to what is now Nunavut.

Capt. William Penny, who sailed from England in May 1850, found evidence of Franklin's winter quarters of 1845–46 on Beechey Island. A number of places are named after Penny, including **Penny Strait**, **Penny Bay**, and the **Penny Ice Cap** on Baffin Island.

Resolute, the second most northern community in Canada, was named after the HMS *Resolute*, which was one of the British ships that came in search of Franklin and wintered here in 1853. **Erebus Bay** and **Terror Bay**, meanwhile, were named for Franklin's own two ships. Erebus was the Greek personification of darkness, while Terror … well, that one speaks for itself.

Charles Francis Hall, an American explorer, led three expeditions to the Arctic. His second journey, of 1864–67, was a search for survivors of the Franklin expedition. During that voyage, Hall camped near the northeastern tip of the Melville Peninsula. The hamlet that is there now was named **Hall's Beach** after this explorer. It is one of the few permanently populated communities north of the Arctic Circle.

Let Me Tell You: Places Named for **Signals** and **Signs**

There's no doubt about it—Canadians are clever. They know there's more than one way to communicate. That's why they have built stone pillars, carved arrows into trees, and yes, even hung bodies on poles. Want to know what all these signals and signs meant? Read on …

From Pillar to Post

The first European fishermen began coming to the coast of Labrador in the sixteenth century. Soon (although no one knows for certain exactly when), they began building stone pillars to act as landmarks for their fishing boats. Where did the fishermen first get the idea to make these stone landmarks? They borrowed it from the Inuit. For centuries, the Inuit had piled up stones to form inuksuit, or "things that can act in the place of a human being." These inuksuit helped show travellers the way home, warned of dangerous places, showed where food was stored, marked a spot where a significant event had occurred, and identified good places for hunting. **Pillar Island**, northeast of Hopedale, was named for the stone pillars that once were found there.

Crime Prevention

A gibbet is an upright post with a wooden arm sticking out. In the nineteenth century, when criminals were often hanged for their misdeeds, bodies would be hung on the gibbet arm so that the public could see them and be persuaded not to repeat their crimes. There is a hill near St. John's, Newfoundland, that used to have a gibbet for just this purpose. Today the hill is still known as **Gibbet Hill**.

Lobstick Landmarks

When early Native peoples wanted to mark a place or an event, they often made a lobstick. This was a spruce or pine tree that had been trimmed in a special way. Natives would climb the tallest, most easily visible tree in an area and cut off all its branches except those at the very top. They then used the tree as a landmark, a talisman, or a monument to a special event. This was common practice among Natives from Newfoundland and Labrador to Alberta, which is why you can find lobstick-inspired place names from one end of this country to the other, including **Lobstick Lake** (in western Labrador, near the Smallwood Reservoir), **Lobstick Bay** (in northern Ontario, on the Lake of the Woods), **Lobstick Narrows** (one in Manitoba, on Kisseynew Lake, and one in Saskatchewan, south of Cumberland House), and just plain ol' **Lobstick** (in Alberta, northeast of Edmonton). Get out your atlas and see how many more you can find!

Save the Trees

No cutting any white pine trees in the king's land in North America! In 1722, the British Parliament passed an act that proclaimed this very thing. Even land that was granted or sold had this prohibition attached. Why? The white pine trees grew tall and straight, and they were to be used only to make masts for the ships of the Royal Navy.

Occasionally, however, the king's surveyor would allow an area of forest to be clear-cut. Before the lumbermen went in with their axes, he would inspect the land, marking any trees that would make good masts with a carving of a broad arrow, the symbol of the Royal Navy. Permission was then given for the slimmer trees, those "unfit for His Majesty's service," to be cut and taken away.

Two places in New Brunswick were named for these practices: **Broad Arrow Brook**, which flows into the Keswick River, and the town of **Kingsclear**, west of Fredericton, where clear-cutting was always allowed.

Calling Long Distance

How did New Brunswick's **Telegraph Hill** get its name? It all started with Prince Edward, a son of George III. He was the military commander-in-chief of the armed forces in New Brunswick and Nova Scotia between 1794 and 1800, and he put in place a semaphore telegraph system between Halifax and Fredericton. (A semaphore system uses different flags as part of an alphabetic code.) A soldier would send a message from the top of a telegraph hill—there were actually seven of these hills in New Brunswick and several others in Nova Scotia—and it would be visible to another solider the next hill along. In this way, messages could be communicated, or "telegraphed," quickly from hill to hill. Although the system was intended for military messages, the prince also sometimes used it to order the punishment of his soldiers!

The Stuff of Legend: Places Named for Local Lore

Many Canadian places got their names because of magical, unbelievable, romantic, or comical events that—according to local stories—occurred there. True or not? Who knows! What we do know is that we sure love to hear the tales told!

Fairy Mischief?

Southwest of Cape George, Nova Scotia, there's a town, now called **Arisaig**, that used to be called Frenchmans Barn. Yes, the name is quite unusual. And so is the explanation for it! There's a huge rock off the coast that looks like—you guessed it—a big barn. Was it once really a barn? And if so, how did it get turned into a rock? Some local residents tell tales to explain this. One of the most popular recounts how, many years ago, the Acadian farmer who owned the barn fell out of favour with the area's fairies. To punish him, they turned his barn into rock—and it has stayed that way ever since.

Side by Side Islands

How did **Billy Island** and **Nan Island**, two small islands in Grand Lake on the New Brunswick–Maine border, get their names? A romantic legend explains that Billy and Nan were canoeing their way to their wedding. The trip across the lake took longer than they thought, however, and night soon came. The two agreed that they should not sleep together before their marriage, so Billy paddled to one island and Nan pulled up her canoe on the one next to it. The islands were later named after this very proper couple!

A Flying Canoe

The name for **Lac de la Chasse-Galerie**, east of Lake Timiskaming, comes from a popular Quebec legend. According to the story, a group of voyageurs were spending the winter in a northern outpost. When the Devil heard them complaining about their loneliness one evening, he approached them with an offer. "I'll put wings on your canoe, and you can fly home and visit your families for one night," he suggested. "But if you speak at all during the flight—even one word—poof!"—he snapped his fingers—"your souls will be mine!"

The voyageurs decided instantly. "We will go," they said, laughing at the thought that they—a group of tough and stoic trappers—might not be able to travel in silence.

Into their canoe they climbed, and into the air they rose. The men paddled, and their *chasse-galerie* took them through the sky, homeward bound. They saw some extraordinary sights as they looked down from that great height, but they bit their lips, determined not to utter even one word to express their amazement.

But when the men saw Montreal and then laid eyes on their very own homes, they couldn't help crying out—and it was then that the Devil snatched them away forever and ever!

(The *chasse* in the word *chasse-galerie* comes from the French verb *chasser,* "to hunt." No one is entirely certain, but it is possible that *galerie* comes from the name of a French nobleman, Sieur de Gallery. Legend has it that when this man was discovered sacrilegiously hunting on a Sunday, he was condemned to track his prey eternally in the skies. This tale might have been adapted for the wilds of Canada!)

Now That's a Temper!

The Huron believed that the giant Kitchikewana protected all of Georgian Bay in Ontario. Taller than today's CN Tower, Kitchikewana wore a tree-stump necklace and a robe made from the pelts of six hundred beavers. But he had a very bad temper, and when he found out that the girl he wanted already had a boyfriend, he dug the fingers of one hand into the ground, creating five bays, and angrily threw the dirt in the air, creating the Thirty Thousand Islands. Then, broken-hearted, Kitchikewana lay down and died, and his followers covered his body with rocks and sand. People say this is why there is an island in Georgian Bay shaped like a prone giant—and that's why they call it **Giants Tomb Island**.

Local Lingo

Saskatchewan is a virtual treasure trove of unusual place names that came about in unusual ways. Take the town of **Ardill**, for example. The story goes that an early English settler was driving his team of horses uphill from the river to this small settlement. "This is an 'ard 'ill to climb!" he said in his British accent, and that's how the town got its name!

There's an equally odd story attached to the community of **Dundurn**. Apparently, a pioneering family in search of new land set out from Winnipeg and began travelling west by cart. They travelled on for weeks and weeks. Finally, with winter approaching, they reached a spot south of present-day Saskatoon that seemed pleasant and fertile. One of the parents, looking around proudly, said, "I think we have done durn well!" Is this really how the town got its name?

A hamlet just west of Saskatoon, meanwhile, got its name when two newlyweds first chose their homestead property. The happy groom exclaimed to his bride, "Isn't this grand, Dora?" And today that town is called **Grandora**!

Want some more? Well, there's a story about a group of settlers from Indiana who settled in the area north of present-day Alsask, near the Alberta-Saskatchewan border, in 1909. The local Native peoples soon began calling these settlers hoosiers, because whenever anyone knocked at their doors, the settlers would call out, "Who's there?" When it came time to choose a name for the town that grew up around the settlement, the answer was obvious: **Hoosier**!

Okay, okay—just one more! In the dry summer of 1913, Nellie McClung, the Canadian novelist and women's rights activist, was taken to visit a green and fertile area just west of Saskatoon. When she saw the lush landscape, she exclaimed, "Superb, an oasis in the desert!" A year later, the name **Superb** was given to the new townsite.

Stop, Thief!

Legend has it that herds of horses used to roam the land near Drumheller, Alberta. They ran free, but they could always be identified because they were branded with the mark of their owners. Still, that didn't mean the horses were completely safe from predators. Local stories tell of animals disappearing into the canyons of the Red Deer River and then reappearing—with different brands! No wonder one of these canyons was given the name **Horse Thief Canyon**.

Another horse thief helped to name a creek northeast of Kimberley, British Columbia. Captured by the Mounties, he was being taken to Fort Steele for trial. "Could I ride a fresh horse?" the thief begged the head constable as the trail went on and on. "Mine is exhausted." All the horses were tired, but the thief persisted and the constable finally agreed. A short while later, the posse reached a creek that ran through a steep gully thick with trees. Seizing the moment, the horse thief yelled to his fresh and prancing mount and sprang away. The officers tried to pursue him, but their horses were simply too tired to run. Before he disappeared altogether, the thief turned to the officers and, with a wave, called, "Ta ta, friends!" Ever since then, this creek has been known as **Ta Ta Creek**.

Who Calls?

The town of **Qu'Appelle**, east of Regina, Saskatchewan, sits on the Qu'Appelle River, which it's named after. *Qu'appelle* is French for "Who calls?" How would a river get this name? Well, it is a translation of Calling River, the name given by local Native peoples. Some people say the Natives often thought they heard the cry of a human coming from the river. They believed that someone's spirit was constantly moving along it, calling out to anyone who passed.

A more romantic explanation points to the legend of a Cree warrior who was paddling home to be wed. Late one night, when he was still days away from his destination, he thought he heard his lover's voice calling to him. How could that be? the young man wondered. It was impossible. He called out, "Who calls? Who calls?" Of course, he got no answer.

When the worried warrior finally returned home, he ran to find his beloved. But she had died. With her last breath, she had called out his name. Had it been her calls that he had heard that night far from home?

A Story of Moose

The city of **Moose Jaw**, also near Regina, gets its name from a nearby creek, the Moose Jaw River, which is a tributary of the Qu'Appelle. There are several explanations for how the river got its unusual name. Some claim that it's simply an English variant on the Cree word *moosegaw*, which means "warm breezes." Others believe it comes from the tale of a wagon breaking down near the river. According to the story, the English lord on board repaired the wagon wheel with the jaw of a moose and then named the river after this handy piece of equipment!

Further Resources

Did we leave out the name of your community? Or has your interest been sparked and you'd like to learn more? Your local library is sure to have many books that will help you uncover additional fascinating Canadian place names. Some of the best we found are these:

Dictionary of Canadian Place Names, Alan Rayburn (Toronto: Oxford University Press, 1977).

Naming Canada, Alan Rayburn (Toronto: University of Toronto Press, 1994).

What's in a Name?, Henry Kelsey Public School (Saskatoon: Western Producer Prairie Books, 1968).

Place Names of Atlantic Canada, William B. Hamilton (Toronto: University of Toronto Press, 1996).

Over 2000 Place Names of Alberta (Expanded Third Edition), Eric J. Holmgren and Patricia Holmgren (Saskatoon: Western Producer Prairie Books, 1976).

British Columbia Place Names, G.P.V. and Helen B. Akrigg (Victoria: Sono Nis Press, 1988).

Alaska-Yukon Place Names, James W. Phillips (Seattle: University of Washington Press, 1973).

If you're technologically inclined, the Internet is also a great resource. It's jam-packed with information-filled Websites like these:

geonames.nrcan.gc.ca/english/Home.html (the Geographical Names Board of Canada)

www.gdbc.gov.bc.ca/bcnames (GeoData B.C., a database of geographical names of British Columbia)

pwnhc.learnnet.nt.ca/databases/geodb.htm (the Geographic Names Database for Northwest Territories)

www.toponymie.gouv.qc.ca/default.asp (the databank of official Quebec place names)

www.ainc-inac.gc.ca/ks/english/2000_e.html (aboriginal place names collected by Indian and Northern Affairs Canada)

www.arctictravel.com/maps/index.html (Nunavut maps and place name translations)

Index of Place Names